Songbook

Authors

Lynn M. Brinckmeyer Texas State University, San Marcos, Texas
Amy M. Burns Far Hills Country Day School, Far Hills, New Jersey
Patricia Shehan Campbell University of Washington, Seattle, Washington
Audrey Cardany University of Rhode Island, Kingston, Rhode Island
Shelly Cooper University of Nebraska at Omaha, Omaha, Nebraska
Anne M. Fennell Vista Unified School District, Vista, California
Sanna Longden Clinician/Consultant, Evanston, Illinois
Rochelle G. Mann Fort Lewis College, Durango, Colorado
Nan L. McDonald San Diego State University, San Diego, California
Martina Miranda University of Colorado, Boulder, Colorado
Sandra L. Stauffer Arizona State University, Tempe, Arizona
Phyllis Thomas Lewisville Independent School District, Lewisville, Texas
Charles Tighe Cobb County School District, Atlanta, Georgia
Maribeth Yoder-White Clinician/Consultant, Banner Elk, North Carolina

 in partnership with 

Boston, Massachusetts
Chandler, Arizona
Glenview, Illinois
New York, New York

ISBN-13: 978-1-4182-6271-6
ISBN-10:   1-4182-6271-4
6 17

Alumot
(Sheaves of Grain)

Harvest Song from Israel
English Words by Sue Ellen LaBelle

Ye - la - dim___ na - gi - la ve - na - sov bim - cho - lot!
Har - vest time has_ come! We'll cir - cle round and dance. Let's re - joice!

Shi - bo - lim___ hiv - shi - lu. Ne' e - sof a - lu - mot!
Sheaves of wheat are_ ripe, We'll sing a song of joy. Raise your voice!

A - lu - mot, shel za - hav, ha - sa - deh ra - chav, ra - chav.
Gold - en sheaves, grain and leaves, We will be the gath - er - ers,

Ba - sa - deh u - va - nir, shi - ru ze - mer la - ka - tsir!
In the field, land's great yield, Let's sing to the har - vest - ers!

Brightly ♩ = c. 132
mf
Eb6
An - oth - er op' - nin', an - oth - er show, ___ in
Eb7
Eb6
Phil - ly, Bos - ton, or Bal - ti - mo'e, ___ a
Eb7
cresc.
Cm7/Eb
Bbdim7/E
Bb7
chance for stage - folks to say "hel - lo," ___ an -
f Eb
C7(b9)
Bmaj7(b5)/F
Bb9
Eb6
mf
oth - er op' - nin' of an - oth - er show. An -
f
mf
oth - er op' - nin' of an - oth - er - er show. An -
Eb6
oth - er job ___ that you hope, at last, ___ will
oth - er job ___ that you hope, at last, ___ will

Another Op'nin', Another Show

Words and Music by Cole Porter
Arranged by Philip Kern

Another Op'nin', Another Show

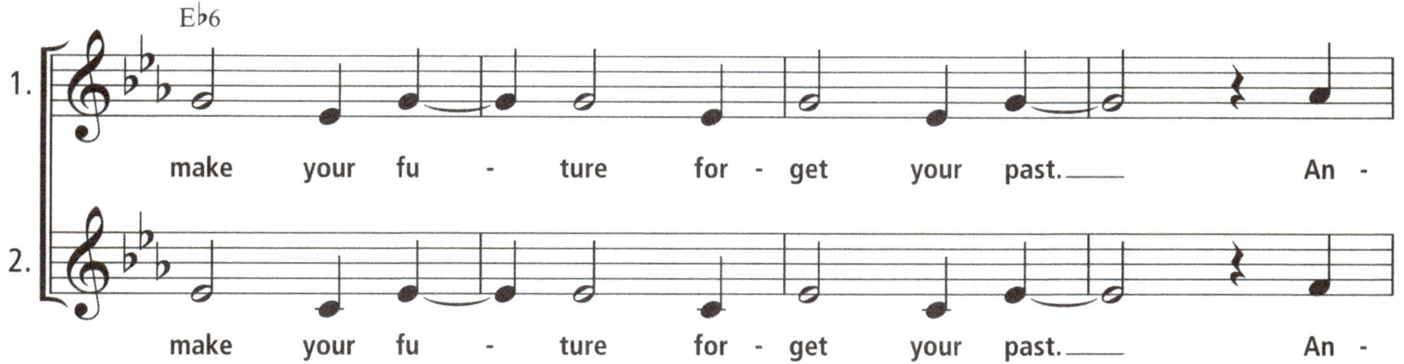

Eb6
make your fu - ture for - get your past.____ An -
make your fu - ture for - get your past.____ An -

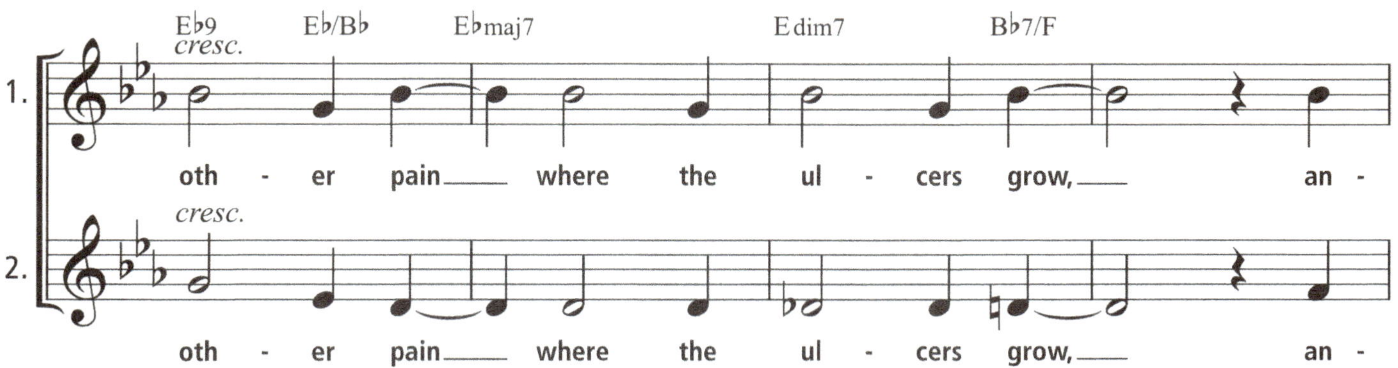

Eb9   Eb/Bb   Ebmaj7   Edim7   Bb7/F
cresc.
oth - er pain____ where the ul - cers grow,____ an -
cresc.
oth - er pain____ where the ul - cers grow,____ an -

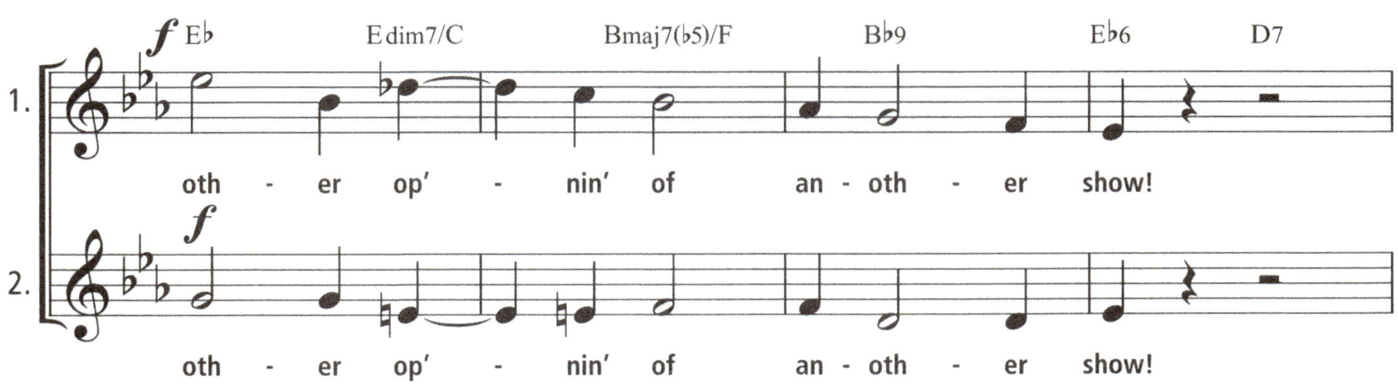

f Eb   Edim7/C   Bmaj7(b5)/F   Bb9   Eb6   D7
oth - er op' - nin' of an - oth - er show!
f
oth - er op' - nin' of an - oth - er show!

mp Gm   D   D7
Four weeks, you re - hearse and re - hearse,
mp
Four weeks, you re - hearse and re - hearse,

Another Op'nin', Another Show

Gm
Eb7/Db Gm/D Eb7 D7
1.
three weeks and it could - n't be worse.
2.
three weeks and it could - n't be worse.

Gm
Gm7/D Em7(b5)/G F7 sub. f
1.
One week, will it ev - er be right? Then
sub. f
2.
One week, will it ev - er be right? Then

Bb Bb/A Bb7/Ab Bb/G Bbdim/Gb Bb mf
1.
out of the hat, it's that big first night! The
mf
2.
out of the hat, it's that big first night! The

Eb6
1.
o - ver - ture is a - bout to start, you
2.
o - ver - ture is a - bout to start, you

Another Op'nin', Another Show

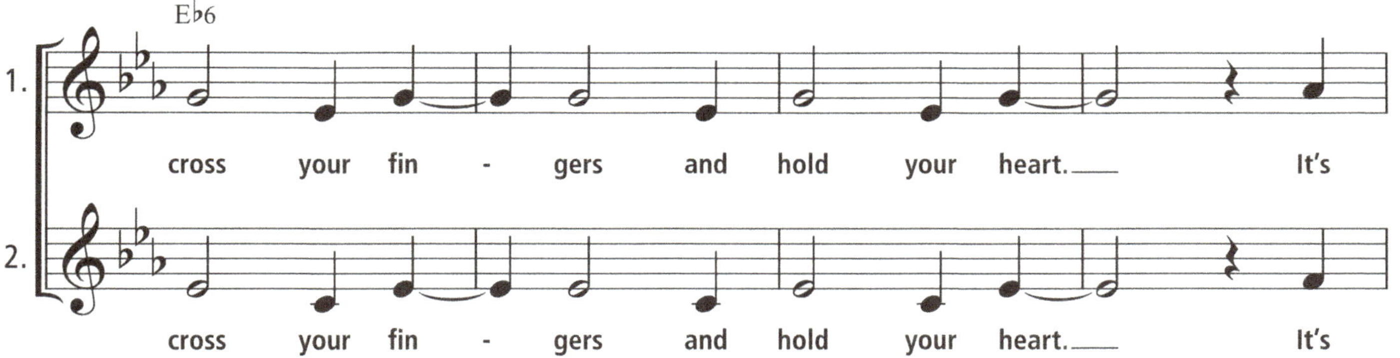

cross your fin - gers and hold your heart.____ It's
cross your fin - gers and hold your heart.____ It's

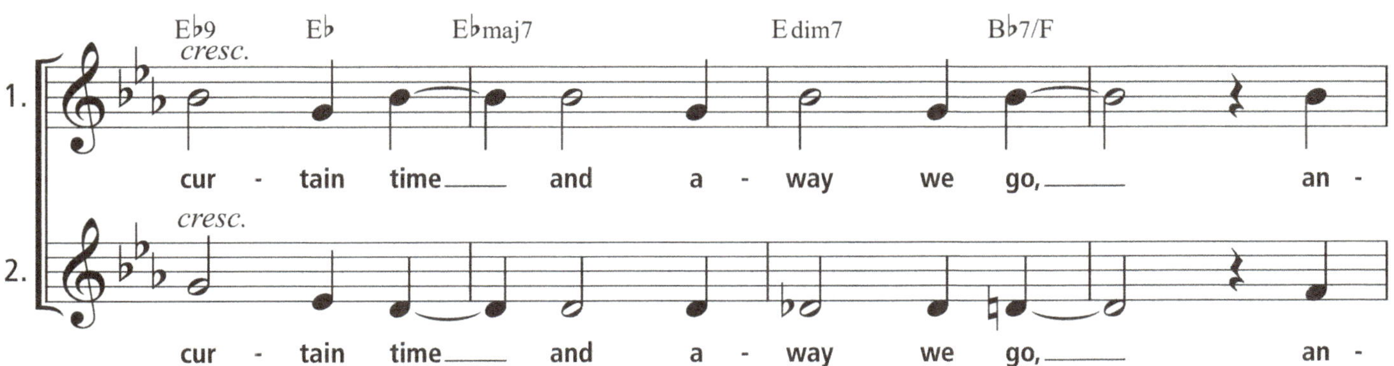

cur - tain time____ and a - way we go,____ an -
cur - tain time____ and a - way we go,____ an -

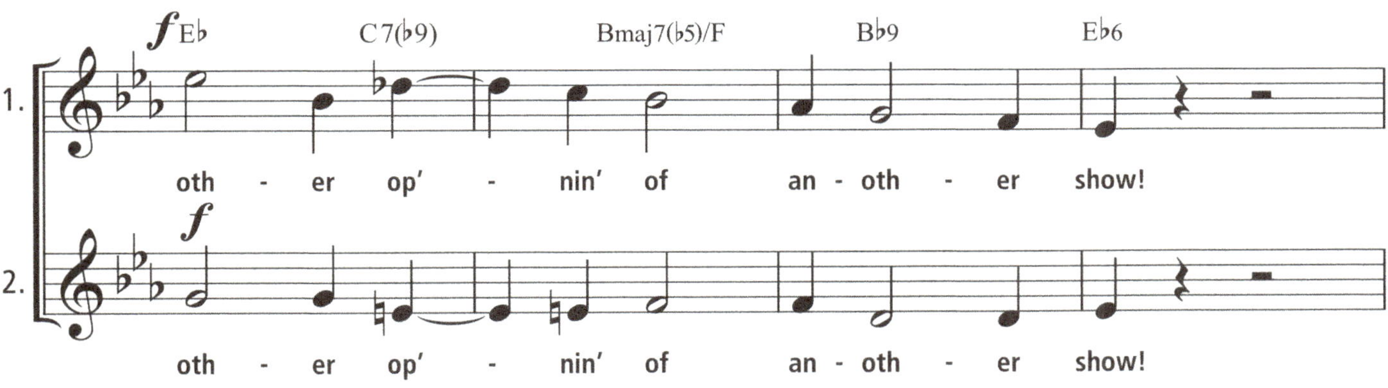

oth - er op' - nin' of an - oth - er show!
oth - er op' - nin' of an - oth - er show!

'Noth - er op' - nin', 'noth - er op' - nin', 'noth - er op' - nin', 'noth - er op' - nin',
An -

Another Op'nin', Another Show

'noth - er op' - nin', 'noth - er op' - nin', 'noth - er op' - nin' night.
oth - er op' - nin', an - oth - er show, in

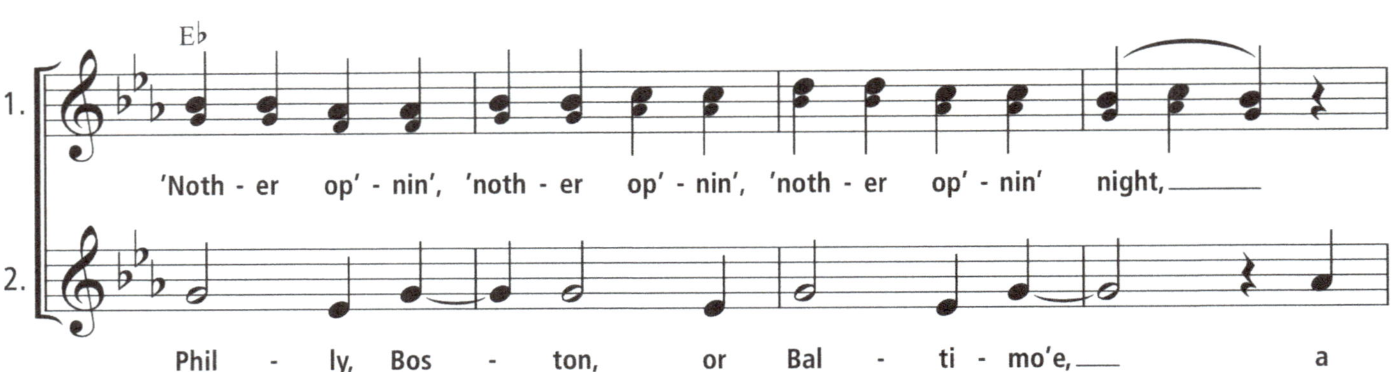

'Noth - er op' - nin', 'noth - er op' - nin', 'noth - er op' - nin' night,
Phil - ly, Bos - ton, or Bal - ti - mo'e, a

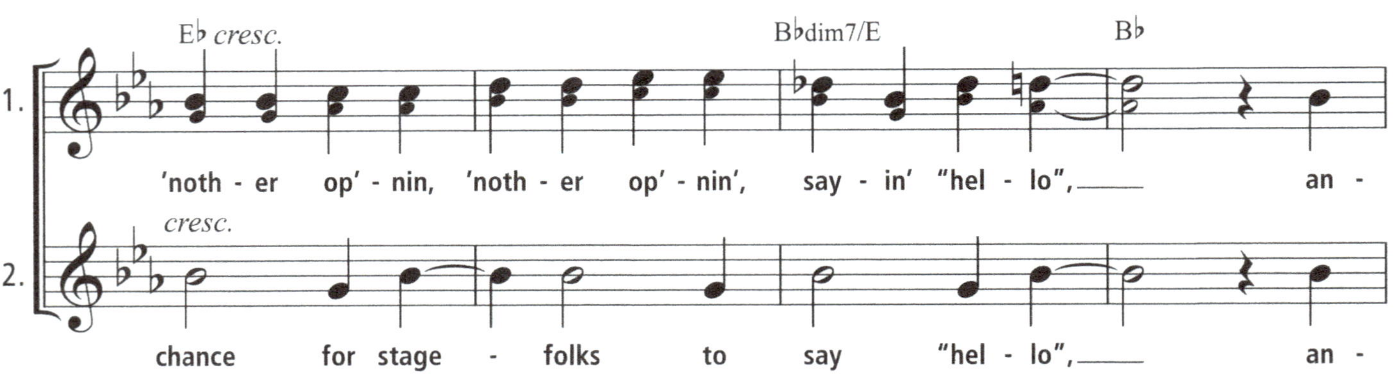

'noth - er op' - nin, 'noth - er op' - nin', say - in' "hel - lo", an -
chance for stage - folks to say "hel - lo", an -

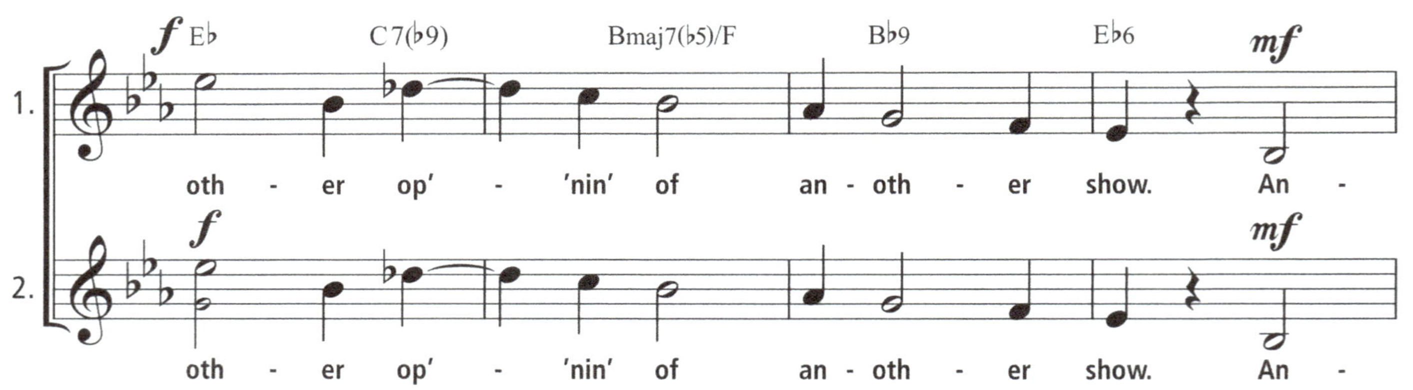

oth - er op' - 'nin' of an - oth - er show. An -
oth - er op' - 'nin' of an - oth - er show. An -

Another Op'nin', Another Show

Eb
Fm7
1.
oth - er job___ that you hope at last,___ will
2.
oth - er op' - nin' night, an -

Eb
Fm7/Bb
1.
make your fu - ture for - get your past.___ An -
2.
oth - er op' - nin' night an -

Ebmaj7
cresc.
Bbdim7
Bb
1.
oth - er pain___ where the ul - cers grow,___ an -
cresc.
2.
oth - er op' - nin' night, an -

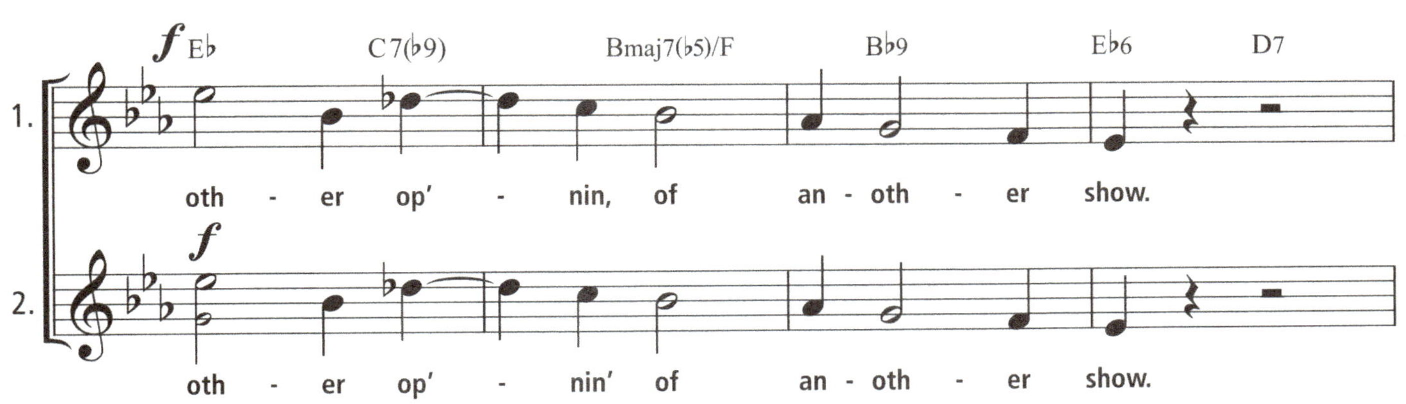

f Eb
C 7(b9)
Bmaj7(b5)/F
Bb9
Eb6
D7
1.
oth - er op' - nin, of an - oth - er show.
f
2.
oth - er op' - nin' of an - oth - er show.

Another Op'nin', Another Show

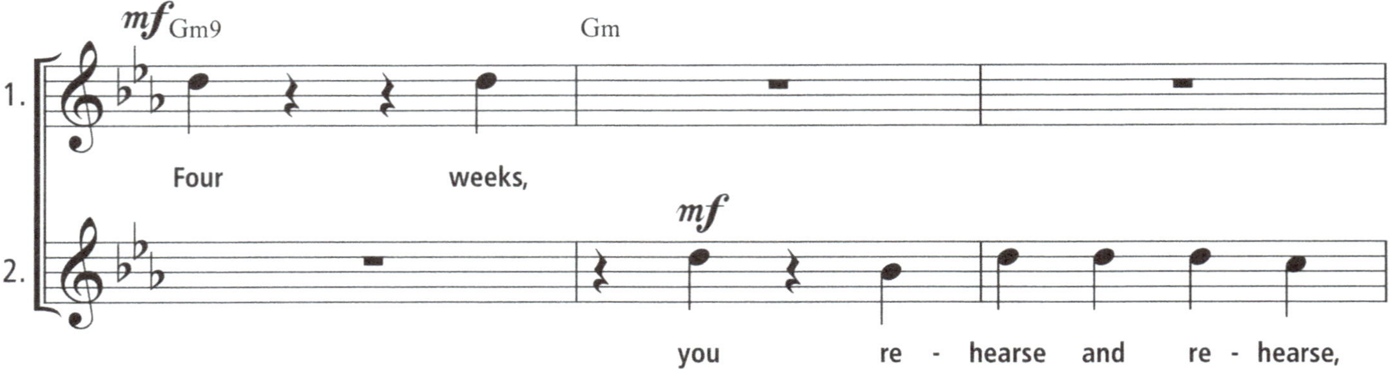

Four weeks,
you re - hearse and re - hearse,

three weeks,
and it could-n't be worse.

One week
will it ev - er be right? Then
Then

out of the hat it's that big first night!
out of the hat it's that big first night!

Another Op'nin', Another Show

N.C.
Dm7/G
1.
Our of the hat,____ it's that
2.
Out of the hat____ it's that big first night.____

Gm7/C
C7
1.
big first night,____ big first night!____ The
2.
Out of the hat____ it's that big first night!____ The

F6
1.
o - ver - ture____ is a - bout to start,____ you
2.
o - ver - ture____ is a - bout to start,____ you

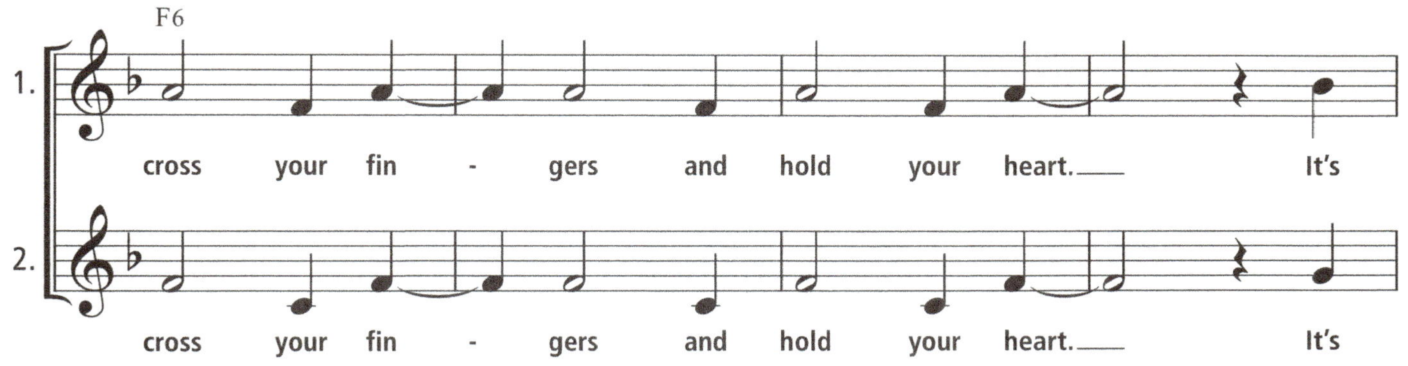

F6
1.
cross your fin - gers and hold your heart.____ It's
2.
cross your fin - gers and hold your heart.____ It's

Another Op'nin', Another Show

F9
F7
Cdim7/F#
C7
1.
cur - tain time______ and a - way we go,______ an -
2.
cur - tain time______ and a - way we go,______ an -

F cresc.
Cdim7/D
Daug7
G7
C7
1.
oth - er op' - nin', just an - oth - er op' - nin' of____
cresc.
2.
oth - er op' - nin' of an -

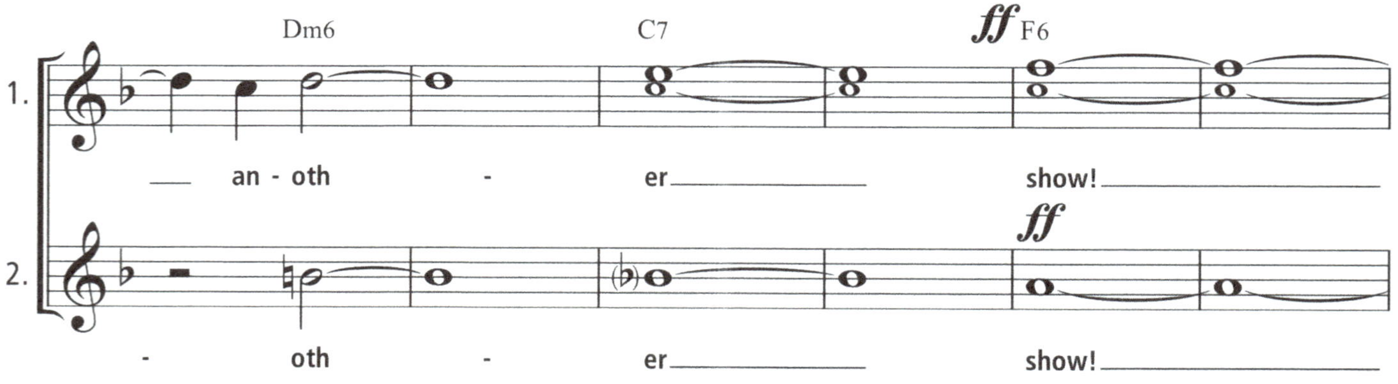

Dm6
C7
ff F6
1.
____ an - oth - er______ show!______
ff
2.
- oth - er______ show!______

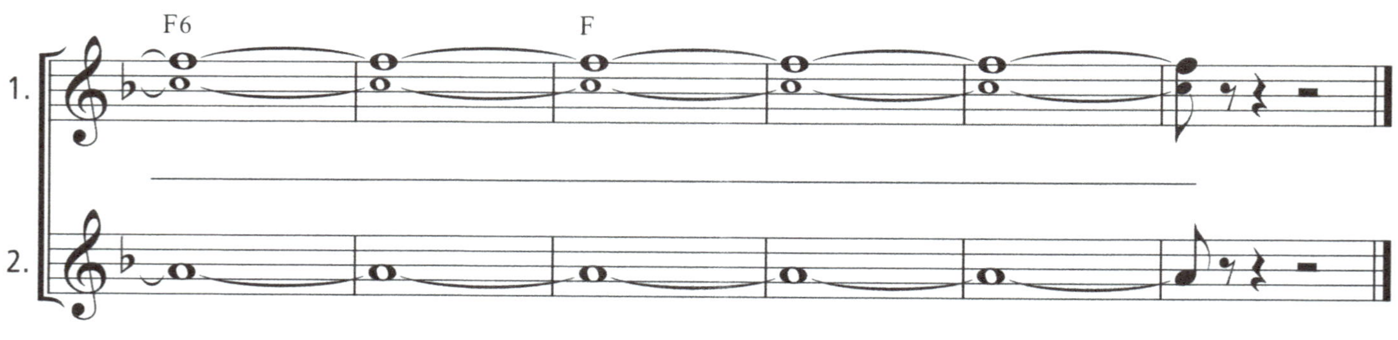

F6
F
1.
2.

Bắt kim thang
(Setting Up the Golden Ladder)

Traditional Song from Viet Nam
English Words by Alice Firgau

Bắt kim thang cà lang bí rọ'. Cột qua kèo kèo qua
Set the gold - en lad - der up; Now jump left, then jump

cột. Chú bán dâu qua câu mà té. Chú bán
right. What a sight! A ven - dor falls from the

ê'ch o' lại làm chi. Con le le dánh trô'ng thôi
bridge; an - oth - er calls. The Le Le bird plays trum - pet and

kèn. Con bìm bịp thôi tò tí te tò te.
drum, And the bim bịp bird sings twiddle dee dum.

The Beat Goes On

Words and Music by Sonny Bono
Arranged by Greg Gilpin

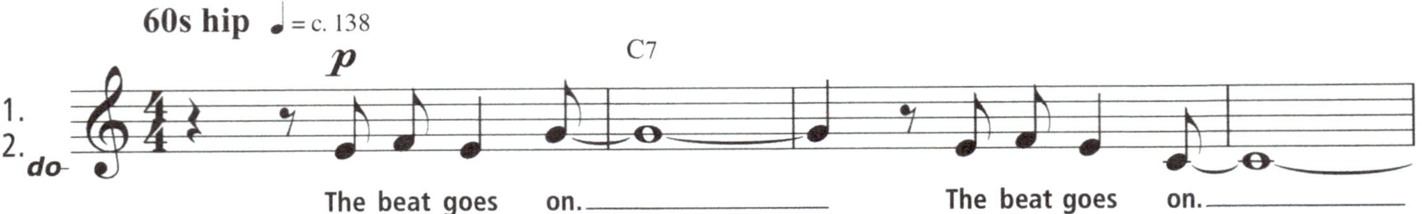
60s hip ♩ = c. 138
p
C7
The beat goes on. The beat goes on.
do

C7
Drums keep pound - ing rhy-thm to the brain.

C7
mp
La da da da dee, la da da da da. The
mel.
La da da da dee, la da da da da.

C7
Charles - ton was once the rage, uh - huh.
mp
Da da dat dwee da da dat

The Beat Goes On

C7
1.
His - to - ry has turned a page, uh - huh. ________ The
2.
Da da dat dwee ___ da da dat The

C7
(vocal slide)
1.
min - i - skirt's the cur - rent thing, uh - huh. ________
2.
min - i - skirt's the cur - rent thing, Da da dat dwee ___ da da dat

mf C7
1.
Tee - ny - bop - per is our new - born king, uh - huh.
mf
2.
Tee - ny - bop - per is our new born king, uh - huh.

N.C. sub. p
C7
1.
And the beat goes on. ________ The beat goes on. ___
p
2.
And the beat goes on. ________

The Beat Goes On

C7
1.
The gro-c'ry store does su-per-mart, uh-huh.
2.
The beat goes on. The gro-c'ry store does su-per-mart.

C7
mp
1.
Lit-tle girls still break
2.
Do do doot dwee do do doot

C7
mf
1.
their hearts, uh-huh. And
mp
mf
2.
Do do doot dwee do do doot And

C7
1.
men still keep on march-ing off to war.
(vocal slide)
2.
men still keep on march-ing off to war.

The Beat Goes On

'Lec - tric - 'lly, they keep their base - ball scores.
'Lec - tric - 'lly, they keep their base - ball scores.

And the beat goes on. The beat goes on.
And the beat goes on.

Drums keep pound - ing
The beat goes on. Drums keep pound - ing

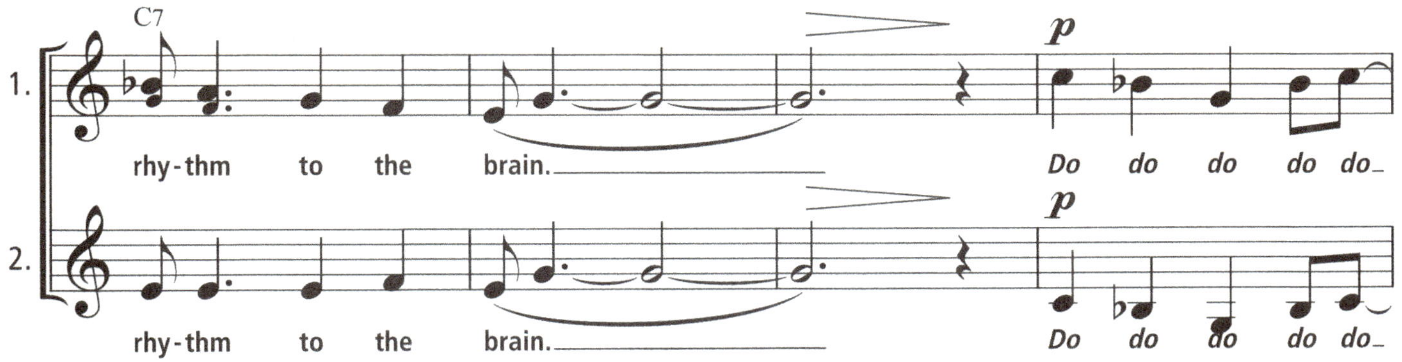
rhy - thm to the brain. Do do do do do
rhy - thm to the brain. Do do do do do

The Beat Goes On

do do do do do do do do do
And the beat goes
do do do do do do do do do
And the beat goes
on. The beat goes on. Ah,
on. The beat goes on. Ah,
mel.
grand - mas sit in chairs and rem - i - nisce.
grand - mas.
(vocal slide)
Bot bot ba da
Bot bot ba da Boys keep chas - ing girls to get a

The Beat Goes On

Ba da bat ba da ba____ ba da bat The cars keep go-ing
kiss. The cars keep go-ing
fast - er all the time,___ fast - er all the time.___
fast - er all the time,___ fast - er all the time.___
Bums still cry.
Bums still cry, "Hey, bud - dy can you spare a dime?"
And the beat goes on,___ on and on,___
And the beat goes on,___ on and on,___

The Beat Goes On

Eb7
Bbm7
1. do ___ and the beat goes on. On and on and
2. do ___ and the beat goes on. On and on and
Eb7
3
1. drums keep pound-ing rhy-thm to the brain.____
mf
2. drums keep pound-ing rhy-thm to the brain.____ La da da da
Eb7
mf
1. La da da da dee.____ La da da da
2. dee.____ La da da da da.
Eb7
mp
1. da. La da da da dee.____
mp
2. La da da da dee.____ La da da da

The Beat Goes On

La da da da da. And the beat goes on.
da. And the beat goes on.

The beat goes on. The beat goes on.
The beat goes on. The beat goes on.

The beat goes on.
The beat goes on.

Do do do do do On!
Do do do do do On!

Blue Mountain Lake

Lumberjack Song from New York
Adapted by Susan Brumfield

Dm
Am
1. Come, all you good fel - lers wher - ev - er you be. Come,
2. There's the Sul - li - van bro - thers and Big Jim - my Lou, And
3. And now, my good fel - lers, a - dieu to you all, For

Dm
C
F
set down a while____ and lis - ten to me. The
old______ Mose Gil - bert and Dan - dy Pat, too. A
Christ - mas is com - ing, I'm going to Glen Falls. And

Dm
Bb
F
C
truth, I will tell you with - out a mis - take, Of the
lot of good fel - lers as ev - er were seen, And they
when I get there, I'll go out on a spree, For you

Dm
Am Dm
rack - ets we had a - round Blue Moun - tain Lake.
all worked for Grif - fin on town - ship nine - teen.
know when I've mon - ey, there's no hold - in' me!
Der - ry

Dm
Am Dm
down, down, down, der - ry down.

Boil Them Cabbage Down

Pioneer Song from the United States

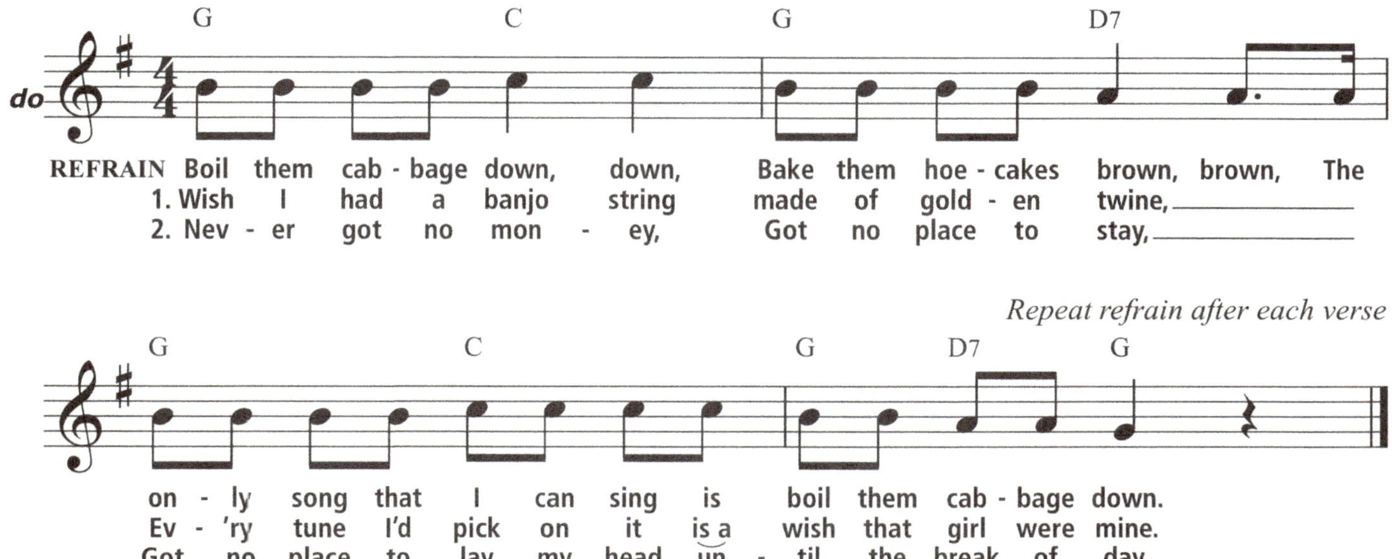

do
G   C   G   D7
REFRAIN Boil them cab - bage down, down, Bake them hoe - cakes brown, brown, The
1. Wish I had a banjo string made of gold - en twine,____
2. Nev - er got no mon - ey, Got no place to stay,____
Repeat refrain after each verse
G   C   G   D7   G
on - ly song that I can sing is boil them cab - bage down.
Ev - 'ry tune I'd pick on it is a wish that girl were mine.
Got no place to lay my head un - til the break of day.

Boil Them Cabbage Down

Recorder Countermelody

Born to Be Somebody

Words and Music by Diane Warren
Arranged by Mike Taylor

A fire that's deep in-side
There's a dream in my soul,
me.
There's a me no one knows,
wait-ing to be set free.
I'm gon-na see that
I'm gon-na see that
day.
day.
I can feel it, I can taste it.
I can feel it, I can taste it.

Born to Be Somebody

F/A
cresc.
Ab
(end solo) f All Voices
Eb
1. Change is com-ing my way.___ I was born_ to be___ some-bod - y.
2. Change is com-ing my way.___ I was born_ to be___ some-bod - y.

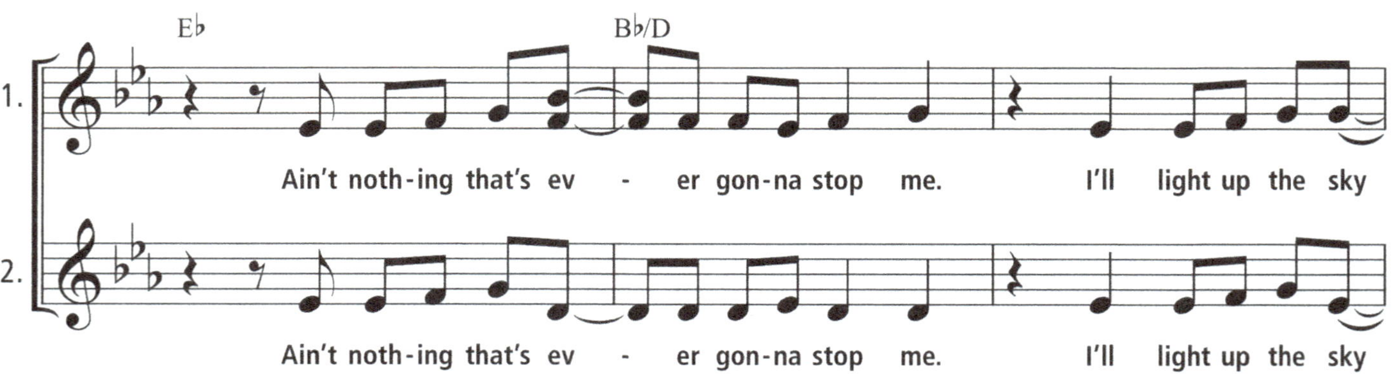

Eb
Bb/D
1. Ain't noth-ing that's ev - er gon-na stop me. I'll light up the sky
2. Ain't noth-ing that's ev - er gon-na stop me. I'll light up the sky

Cm
Bbsus
Ab
G7
1. ___ like light - ning. show 'em what_ I am made of._
2. ___ like light - ning. I'm_ gon-na rise a-bove,

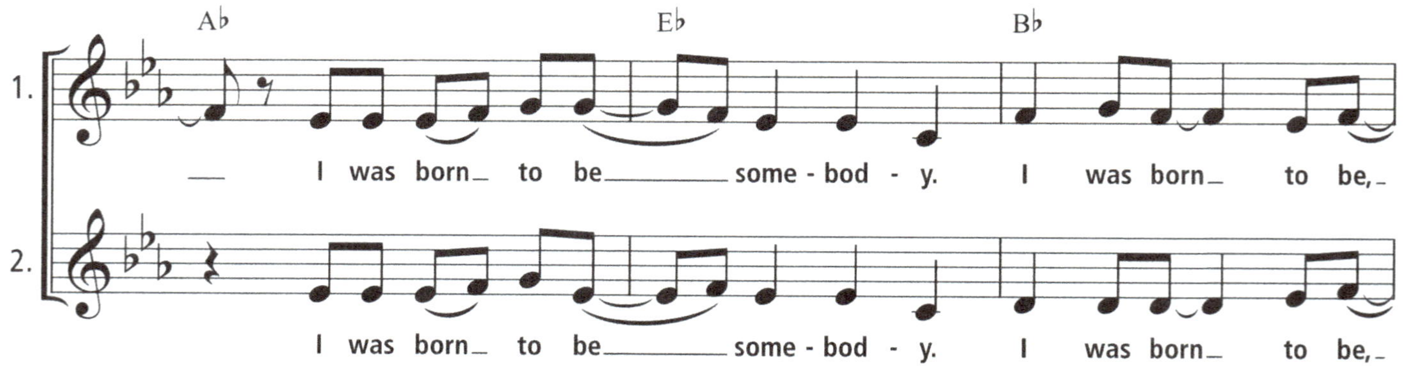

Ab
Eb
Bb
1. ___ I was born_ to be___ some-bod - y. I was born_ to be,_
2. I was born_ to be___ some-bod - y. I was born_ to be,_

Born to Be Somebody

Fm
A♭
A♭(add9)
1.
and this world will be-long to me.
2.
and this world will be-long to me.

E♭
B♭
mf
Cm
1.
This world can make you feel
mf
2.
This life can kick you a - round.

Cm
E♭
B♭
1.
small.
2.
But they will not keep me down.

Cm
Fm
1.
I was born to stand tall.
I'm go-ing all the
2.
I'm go-ing all the

Born to Be Somebody

1. way.___ I can feel it, I be - lieve it.
2. way.___ I can feel it, I be - lieve it.
1. I'm here, I'm here to stay.___ I was born___ to be___ some - bod - y.
2. I'm here, I'm here to stay.___ I was born___ to be___ some - bod - y.
1. Ain't noth-ing that's ev - er gon-na stop me. I'll light up the sky___
2. Ain't noth-ing that's ev - er gon-na stop me. I'll light up the sky___
1. ___ like light - ning. Show 'em what___ I am made of.___
2. ___ like light - ning. I'm___ gon-na rise a-bove.

Born to Be Somebody

Ab   Eb   Bb
1. I was born to be some-bod-y. I was born to be,
2. I was born to be some-bod-y. I was born to be,

Fm   Ab   Cm7
1. and this world will be-long to me. Feel it,
2. and this world will be-long to me. Feel it,

Bb
1. be-lieve it, dream it, be it.
2. be-lieve it, dream it, be it.

Bb   F
1. I was born to be some-bod-y.
2. I was born to be some-bod-y.

Born to Be Somebody

F
C/E
1.
do
Ain't noth-ing that's ev - er gon-na stop me.
I'll light up the sky
2.
do
Ain't noth-ing that's ev - er gon-na stop me.
I'll light up the sky

Dm
F/C
B♭
A7
1.
______ like light - ning.
Show 'em what_ I am made of._
2.
______ like light - ning.
I'm__ gon-na rise a-bove.

B♭
F
C
1.
__ I was born_ to be______ some - bod - y.
I was born_ to be,_
2.
I was born_ to be______ some - bod - y.
I was born_ to be,_

Gm
B♭
1.
______
and this world will be-long____ to me.___
2.
______
and this world will be-long____ to me.___

Born to Be Somebody

Dm7
C/E
Oh, oh, oh, oh.
Oh, oh, oh, oh.
Gm
F/A
B♭
F
And this world will be-long to me.
And this world will be-long to me.
F
C/E
Gm rit.
F/A
Yeah, yeah, oh. And
Yeah, yeah, oh. And
Slower
B♭sus2
this world will be-long to me.
this world will be-long to me.

A Brand New Day

Words and Music by Luther Vandross

REFRAIN
Can't you feel a brand new day?
Last time, repeat ad lib
Can't you feel a brand new day?
VERSE
1. Ev - 'ry - bod - y look a - round 'cause there's a
2. Ev - 'ry - bod - y be glad be - cause the
rea - son to re - joice, you see.
sun is shin - ing just for us.
Ev - 'ry - bod - y come out and let's com -
Ev - 'ry - bod - y wake up in - to the
mence to sing - ing joy - ful - ly.
morn - ing in - to hap - pi - ness.
Ev - 'ry - bod - y look up and feel the
Hel - lo world, it's like a

A Brand New Day

Ab/Bb   Eb/Bb   Bb
hope that we've been wait - ing for.
dif - f'rent way of liv - ing now.
Bb   F/Bb
Ev - 'ry - bod - y be glad because our
Thank you, world, I al - ways
Ab/Bb   Eb/Bb   Bb
si - lent fear and dread are gone.
knew that we'd be free some - how.
C   G/C
Free - dom, you see, has got our
In har - mo - ny, let's show the
Bb/C   F/C   C
hearts sing - ing so joy - ful - ly.
world that we've got lib - er - ty.
C   G/C
Just look a - bout, you owe it
It's such a change for us to
Bb/C   F/C   C   D.C.
to your - self to check it out.
live so in - de - pen - dent - ly.

By the Waters of Babylon

Caribbean Folk Song
Words from Psalm 137

(Add harmony part on D.C. only)
By the wa-ters of Bab - y - lon, Where we sat down,
And there we wept when we re-mem - bered Zi - on.
But the wick - ed car - ry us a - way cap - tiv - i - ty, Re -
quire of us a song. How can you sing the Lord's
own song in a strange land?

Canto del agua
(Song of the Water)

Joropo from Venezuela
English Words by Alice Firgau

1. Es un can - to ma - ña - ne - ro_____ a la o -
1. You can hear me sing_ a love song_____ as I

ri - lli - ta_ del rí - o._____ Es un can - to ma - ña -
stand be - side_ the riv - er._____ You can hear me sing_ a

ne - ro_____ a la o - ri - lli - ta_ del rí - o. Que te
love song_____ as I stand be - side_ the riv - er. In the

va di - cien - do, ne - gra, tá - pa - me que ten - go frí - o. Que te
ear - ly morn - ing hours,_ feel-ing cold, I sing_ and shiv - er. In the

va di - cien - do, ne - gra, va - ma - nos a e - na - mo - rar._____
ear - ly morn - ing hours,_ feel-ing cold, I sing_ and shiv - er._____

Canto del agua

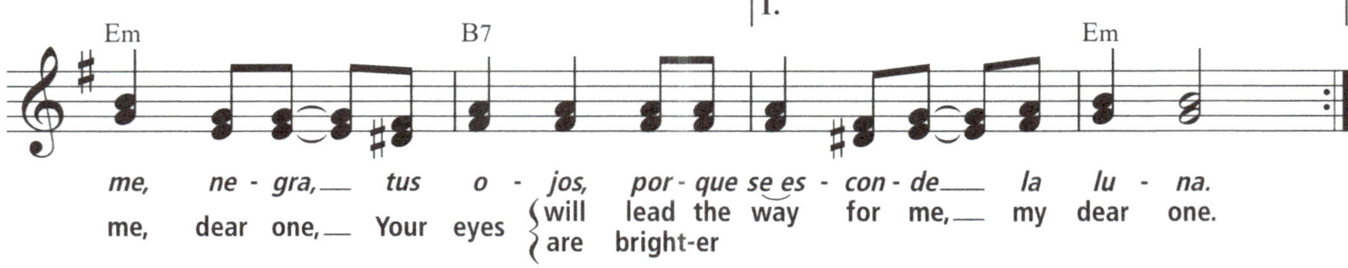

2. Ay yai yai es - ta no - che yo___ me voy,
3. Ay yai yai yo no sé lo que___ me pa - sa,
2. Ay yai yai for to - night I'll roam___ the dunes,
3. Ay yai yai when I'm there out by___ the sea,

Ay yai yai a pa - sear - me en-tre___ las du - nas,
Ay yai ayi cuan - do es - toy cer - ca___ del mar.___
Ay yai yai by the light of the___ full moon.___
Ay yai yai there's a spell comes o - ver me.___

Ay yai yai prés - ta - me, ne - gra,___ tus o - jos, prés - ta -
Ay yai yai stay by me, dear one,___ I need you close to

1.
me, ne - gra,___ tus o - jos, por - que se es - con - de___ la lu - na.
me, dear one,___ Your eyes {will lead the way for me,___ my dear one.
                           {are bright-er

2.
se es - con - de___ la lu - na.
than the wan - ing moon - light.

Fine (last time)   D.S. al Fine

Come Back, Liza
(Watah Come a Me Eye)

Jamaican Folk Song
Arranged, with New Words and Music,
by Sally K. Albrecht and Jay Althouse

1st time: PART 1 only
2nd time: PART 2 only
3rd time: Sing both parts

Ev-'ry time I 'mem-ber Li-za, wa-tah come a me eye.*
Oh, my Li-za make me cry. When I think of her, my, oh, my.

When I think a-bout my Li-za, wa-tah come a me eye.
I re-mem-ber her good-bye. When I think of it, make-a me sigh.

Come back Li-za, come back, gal. Wa-tah come a me
Come back, come back Li-za. Come on back,

* Water comes to my eyes - I cry!

Come Back, Liza

C
1. eye. Come back Li - za, come back, gal.
2. don't make me cry. Come back, come back Li - za,

G
C
(repeat twice)
1. Wa - tah come a me eye.
2. wa - tah, wa - tah, come a me eye.

G
C
1. Wa - tah come a me eye.
2. Wa - tah, wa - tah, come a me eye.

Corta la caña
(Head for the Canefields)

Folk Song from Puerto Rico
English Words by Aura Kontra

Yo ven-go de mon-te a - den - tro de cor-tar ca - ña, ca - ñe-
I work in the su - gar cane - fields, The crop that I bear is heav-

- ro, por más ca - ña que se cor - te nun - ca se ga-na el di - ne-
- y, No mat-ter how much I car - ry it will nev - er bring much mon -

- ro. To-do el mun-do la pro-cla - ma que es muy fá-cil de cor -
- ey. Some say it's an ea-sy liv - ing, cut-ting su-gar all day

tar, cuan-do se ja-la la mo - cha na-die quie-re tra-ba-jar.
long. When-ev-er a hand is need - ed no one wants to come a-long.

Cor - ta la ca - ña, ca - ñe - ro, cór - ta la.
Head for the cane - fields each morn-ing, cut them down.

Cor - ta la ca - ña, ca - ñe - ro, cór - ta la.
Head for the cane - fields till sun-set, cut them down.

Cowboys' Christmas Ball

Cowboy Song from the United States
Lyrics from a poem by Larry Chittenden (1893)

1. Way out in west - ern Tex - as, where the Clear Fork's wa - ters
2. The mu - sic was a fid - dle and a live - ly tam - bour -
3. The lead - er was a fel - ler that came from Swen - son's
4. "Sa - loot yer love - ly crit - ters, now swing and let 'em

flow, Where the cat - tle are a - brows - in' and the
ine, And a vi - ol came, im - port - ed by the
ranch, They called him Win - dy Bil - ly from
go; Climb the grape - vine round 'em; now

Span - ish po - nies grow; Where the an - te - lope is
stage from Ab - i - lene. The room was togged out
Lit - tle Dead Man's Branch, His rig was kind - a
all hands do - si - do; You mave - rick, join the

graz - in' and the lone - ly plov - ers call, It was
gor - geous with mis - tle - toe and shawls, And the
care - less, big spurs and high - heled boots; He
round - up. Now rope and bal - ance all!" Hi!

there that I at - tend - ed the cow - boys' Christ - mas ball.
can - dles flick - ered fes - tious a - round the air - y hall.
had the rep - u - ta - tion that comes when fel - lers shoot.
It was get - tin' ac - tive at the cow - boys' Christ - mas ball.

Dancing Queen
(from Mamma Mia!)

Words and Music by
Benny Andersson, Stig Anderson
and Björn Ulvaeus
Arranged by Alan Billingsley

Disco ♩ = 96-100
do
do
Ah
Ah
ah
ah
ah
ah
ah
ah
oh
oh

Dancing Queen

D/F#
A/E
E
1.
2.
yeah.
You can dance,
3.
yeah.
You can dance,

C#7
C#aug
F#m
1.
2.
you can ji - (h)ive, hav - ing the time of your
3.
you can ji - (h)ive, hav - ing the time of your

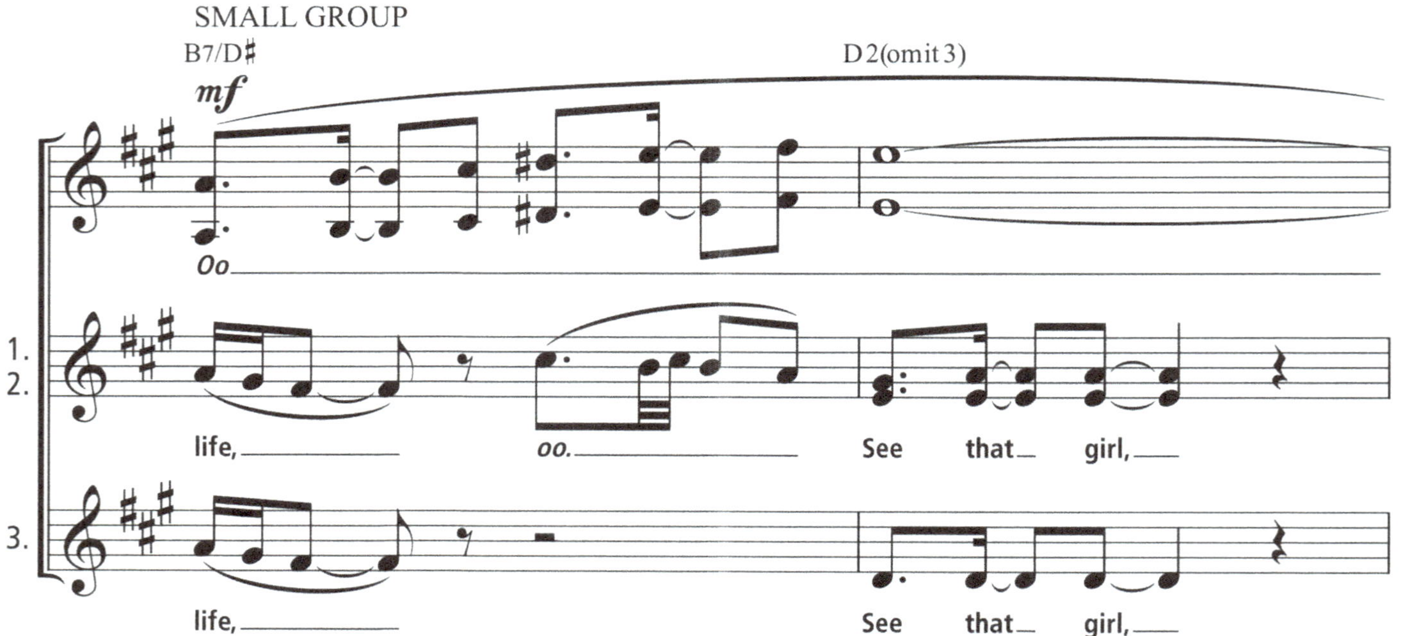

SMALL GROUP
B7/D#
D2(omit 3)
mf
Oo
1.
2.
life, oo. See that girl,
3.
life, See that girl,

Dancing Queen

D 2(omit 3)/B
E7sus
A
yeah.
watch that scene, dig-gin' the danc - ing queen.
watch that scene, dig-gin' the danc - ing queen.

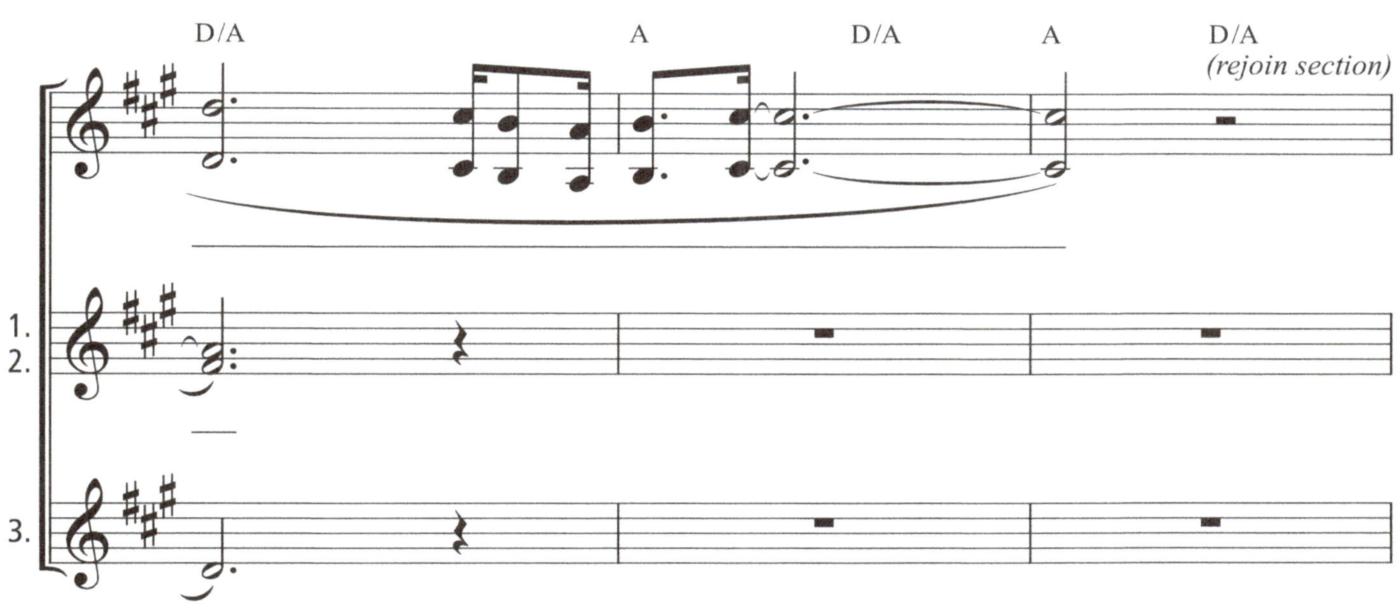

D/A
A
D/A
A
D/A
(rejoin section)

Dancing Queen

Fri - day night_ and the lights are low,____
Fri - day night_ and the lights are low,____
Look - ing out_ for a place to go.____ Oh,____
Look - ing out_ for a place to go.____ Oh,____
where they play_ the right mu - sic, get - ting in_ the swing, you've come to
where they play_ the right mu - sic, get - ting in_ the swing, you've come to
look for a king.____
look for a king.____

Dancing Queen

A
D/A
1.
2.
An - y - bod - y could be that guy;___
You're a teas - er, you turn 'em on;
3.
An - y - bod - y could be that guy;___
You're a teas - er, you turn 'em on;

A
F#m
1.
2.
night is young and the mu - sic's high.___
leave 'em burn - ing and then you're gone.___
3.
night is young and the mu - sic's high.___
leave 'em burn - ing and then you're gone.___

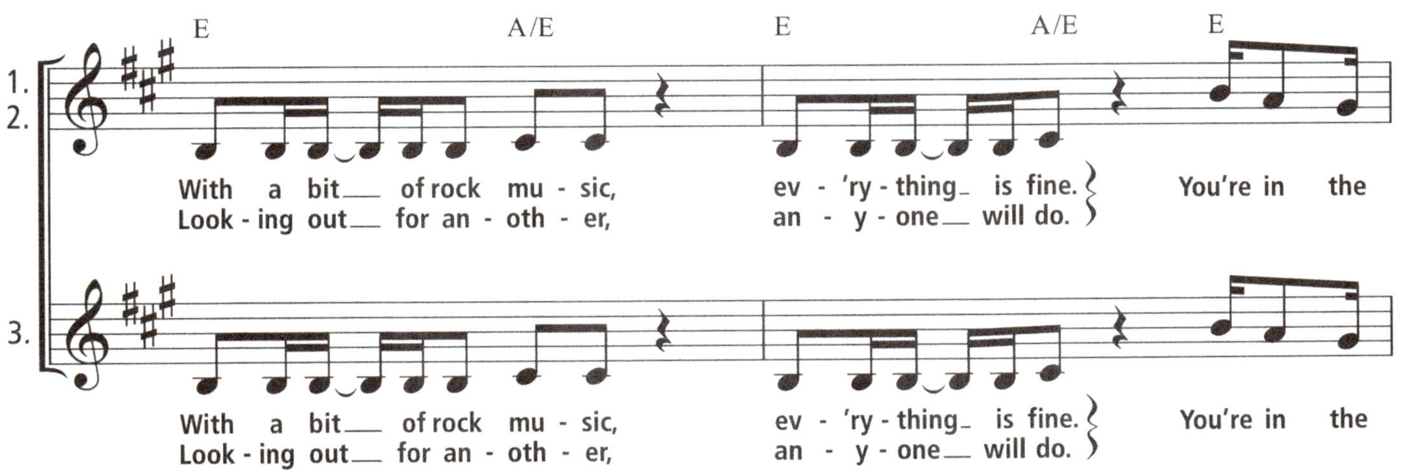

E
A/E
E
A/E
E
1.
2.
With a bit__ of rock mu - sic, ev - 'ry - thing__ is fine. You're in the
Look - ing out__ for an - oth - er, an - y - one__ will do.
3.
With a bit__ of rock mu - sic, ev - 'ry - thing__ is fine. You're in the
Look - ing out__ for an - oth - er, an - y - one__ will do.

Dancing Queen

E   F#m   E   F#m
mood   for   a   dance.____   And   when   you
mood   for   a   dance.____   And   when   you
Bm7   E   E7
get   the   chance,   you   are   the
get   the   chance,   you   are   the
A   D/A   A
danc - ing   queen,   young   and   sweet   on - ly   sev - en - teen.____
danc - ing   queen,   young   and   sweet   on - ly   sev - en - teen.____
D   A   D/A
____   Danc - ing   queen,   feel   the   beat   from   the
____   Danc - ing   queen,   feel   the   beat   from   the

Dancing Queen

tam - bou - rine, ___ oh yeah. ___
tam - bou - rine, ___ oh yeah. ___
You ___ can dance, ___ you ___ can ji - (h)ive,
You ___ can dance, ___ you ___ can ji - (h)ive,
Oo ___
hav - ing ___ the time of ___ your life, ___ oo. ___ See that ___ girl, ___
hav - ing ___ the time of ___ your life, ___ See that ___ girl, ___

Dancing Queen

D 2(omit 3)/B
E7sus
A
yeah.
watch that scene, dig-gin' the danc - ing queen.
watch that scene, dig-gin' the danc - ing queen.
1.
2.
3.

1.
D/A
A
D/A
1.
2.
3.

Dancing Queen
A   D/A   A   D/A   2. A
1. 2.
3.
D/A   A   D/A
Oh.
Dig - gin' the danc - ing___ queen.
Dig - gin' the danc - ing___ queen.
A   D/A   Amaj9   A
Dig - gin' the danc - ing___ queen!
Dig - gin' the danc - ing___ queen!

Ding-Dong! The Witch Is Dead

Music by Harold Arlen
Lyrics by E.Y. Harburg
Arranged by Debbie Cavalier

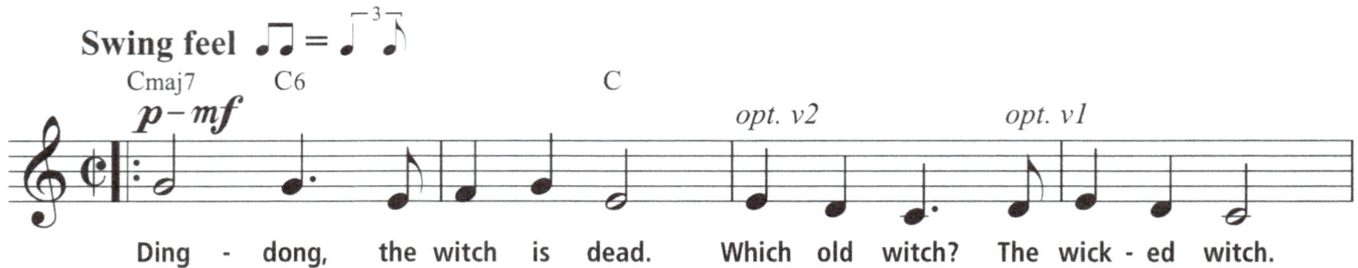

Swing feel
Ding - dong, the witch is dead. Which old witch? The wick - ed witch.

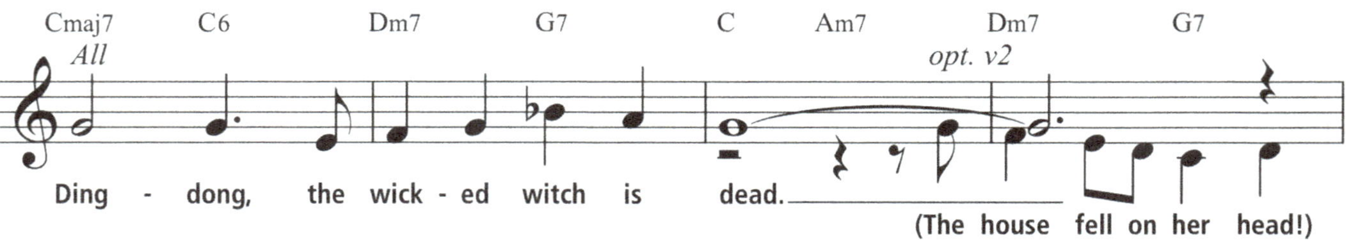

Ding - dong, the wick - ed witch is dead.
(The house fell on her head!)

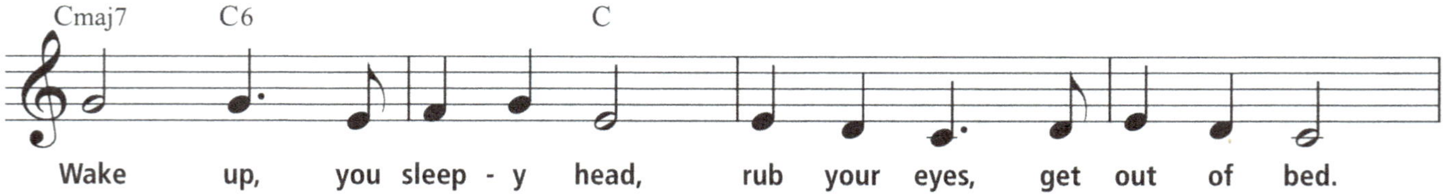

Wake up, you sleep - y head, rub your eyes, get out of bed.

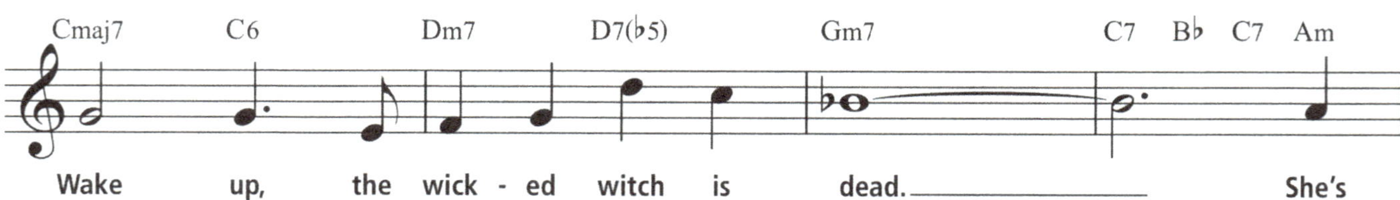

Wake up, the wick - ed witch is dead. She's

gone where the gob - lins go be - low, be - low, be - low. Yo -

Ding-Dong! The Witch Is Dead

Gmaj7   G6   Em7/A Am7   D6   Dm7/G   G7
opt. v2
ho,   let's   o - pen   up   and   sing   and   ring   the bells   out.

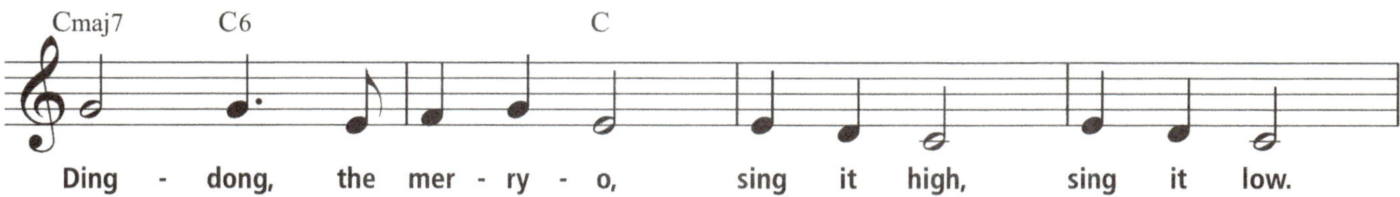

Cmaj7   C6   C
Ding - dong,   the   mer - ry - o,   sing   it   high,   sing   it   low.

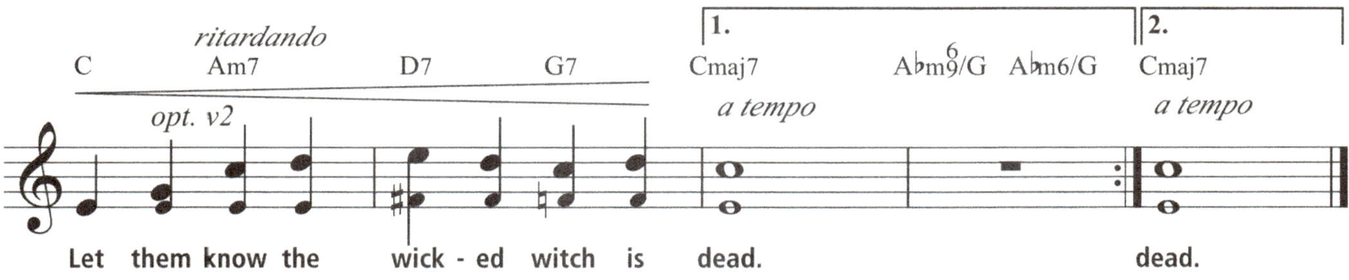

ritardando
C   Am7   D7   G7   Cmaj7   Abm9/G Abm6/G   Cmaj7
opt. v2
1.
a tempo
2.
a tempo
Let   them know the   wick - ed   witch   is   dead.   dead.

A Distant Shore
(A Partner Song with "The Water Is Wide")

Traditional Folk Song
Arranged, with New Words and Music,
by Mary Donnelly and George L.O. Strid

PART 2 (or unis.)
Once I gazed up-on a dis-tant shore,
watch-ing sea birds as they filled the sky.
Stand-ing out there in the mist-y air, how I
wished that I could fly.
PART 1 (or unis.)
slight rit.
a tempo
The wa-ter is wide;
I can-not cross o'er. And nei-ther have I

A Distant Shore

Em   F   D   G
the wings to fly. Give me a boat

G   D
that can car - ry two,   and both shall row,

D   G   2
my love and I.

D D7 Dsus4 D7 G
PART 1 mf   slight rit.   a tempo
The wa-ter is wide;   I can-not cross o'er.

PART 2   mf
Once I gazed up - on a dis - tant

G   Em   F
And nei-ther have I   the wings to fly.

shore,   watch - ing sea birds as they filled the

A Distant Shore

D   G
1. Give me a boat that can car - ry two,
2. sky.   Stand - ing out there in the mist - y

G   D   G
1. and both shall row, my love and I. How I
2. air, how I wished that I could fly. How I

D   G a tempo   rit.
decresc.   rit.   mp
1. wish that both shall row, my love and I.
decresc.   mp
2. wished that I could fly.

A Distant Shore
(A Partner Song with "The Water Is Wide")
Recorder Countermelody

Dona nobis pacem

Traditional Canon

I
do
G   D7   G   D
Do - na no - bis pa - cem, pa - cem,
C   G   D   G
Do - na no - bis pa - cem.
II
G   D7   G   D
Do - na no - bis pa - cem,
C   G   D   G
Do - na no - bis pa - cem.
III
G   D7   G   D
Do - na no - bis pa - cem,
C   G   D   G
Do - na no - bis pa - cem.

Down by the Riverside

African American Spiritual
Arranged by Addie Brown

VERSE
G
1. Gon - na   lay   down   my   sword and   shield
2. Gon - na   join hands   with   ev - 'ry - one___
3. Gon - na   ring out   a   song of   joy___
Down   by   the

G
D7
G
riv - er - side, ___   Down   by   the   riv - er - side, ___   Down   by   the

G
riv - er - side, ___   Gon-na lay down   my   sword and   shield
                        Gon-na join hands   with ev - 'ry - one___
                        Gon-na ring out   a   song of   joy___
Down   by   the

Down by the Riverside

G
D7
G
1.
2.
riv - er - side And stud-y war no more.

REFRAIN
C
Cm
1.
2.
I ain't gon - na stud - y war no more, I ain't gon - na

G
D7
1.
2.
stud-y war no more, I ain't gon-na stud-y war no

1.
G
2.
G
1.
2.
more, I ain't gon - na more.

Down in the Valley

Folk Song from Kentucky

do
D
A7
D
A7
D

1. Down in the val - ley, the val - ley so
2. Build me a cas - tle for - ty feet
3. Writ - ing a let - ter con - tain - ing three

low, Hang your head o - ver, hear the wind
high, So I can see you as you pass
lines, An - swer my ques - tion: "Will you be

blow. Hear the wind blow, dear, hear the wind
by. As you pass by, dear, as you pass
mine?" Will you be mine, dear, will you be

blow, Hang your head o - ver, hear the wind blow.
by, So I can see you as you pass by.
mine? An - swer my ques - tion: "Will you be mine?"

El carnavalito humahuaqueño
(The Little Humahuacan Carnival)

Folk Song from Argentina
English words by Donald Kalbach

1. Lle - gan-do es-tá el_ car-na - val, que-bra-de - ño mi__ cho-li - ta.
2. La la la la__ la la la, la la la la la__ la la la.
1. The car - ni - val__ has be - gun, so be hap - py, my_ dear-est one.
2. La la la la__ la la la, la la la la la__ la la la.
Lle - gan-do está el_ car-na - val, que-bra-de - ño mi__ cho-li - ta.
La la la la__ la la la, la la la la la__ la la la.
The car - ni - val__ has be - gun, so be hap - py, my_ dear-est one.
La la la la__ la la la, la la la la la__ la la la.
Fies - ta de la que - bra - da hu-ma-hua - que - ña pa - ra can - tar.
Fes - ti-val from que - bra - da, Come to the par - ty and sing and play.
Er - que, cha-ran - go y bom - bo car-na-val - i - to pa - ra bai - lar.
Horns and gui - tars and drums put joy in your step as you dance to - day.
Coda
lar.
day.
Bom - bo-ro bom bom, bom-bo-ro bom bom, bom-bo-ro bom bom bom.

El carnavalito humahuaqueño
(The Little Humahuacan Carnival)
Recorder Countermelody

Ezekiel Saw the Wheel

African American Spiritual

REFRAIN
E - ze-kiel__ saw the wheel, 'Way up in the mid-dle of the air, E -
ze-kiel__ saw the wheel, 'Way in the mid-dle of the air. Now the
big wheel turn by faith, And the lit - tle wheel turn by the
grace of God, It's a wheel in a wheel, 'Way in the mid-dle of the air.
VERSE
1. Some go to church for to sing and shout, 'Way in the middle of the air, Be -
2. One of these days 'bout_ twelve o' - clock,
fore six months they're shout - ed out! 'Way in the mid-dle of the air.
This old world gonna reel and rock!
Fine
D.C. al Fine

Flip, Flop and Fly

*Words and Music by Charles Calhoun
and Lou Willie Turner*

Swing style
VERSE
D
do
1. Now when I get the blues I get me a rock - in' chair, __
2. Now when I get __ lone-some I jump on the tel - e - phone, _

D
G
D
When I get the blues I get me a rock - in' chair. __
When I get __ lone-some I jump on the tel - e - phone, _

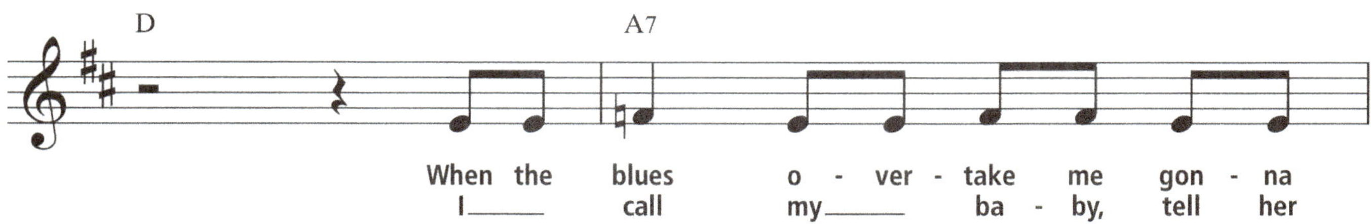

D
A7
When the blues o - ver - take me gon - na
I __ call my __ ba - by, tell her

G
D
rock right a - way from here. __
I'm on my way back home. __

Flip, Flop and Fly

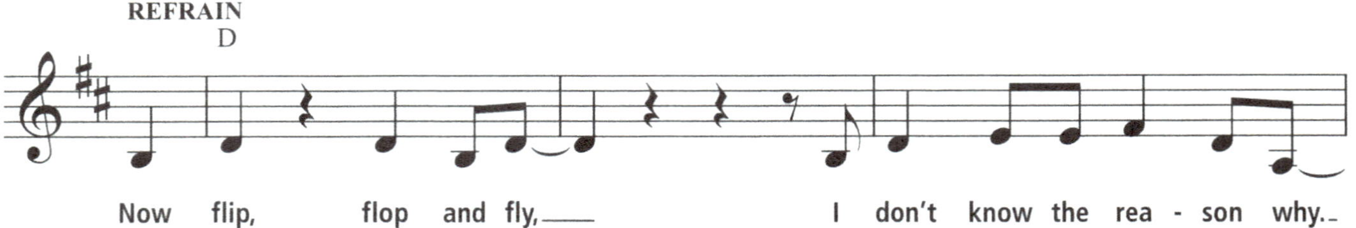

REFRAIN
D
Now flip, flop and fly,____ I don't know the rea - son why.__

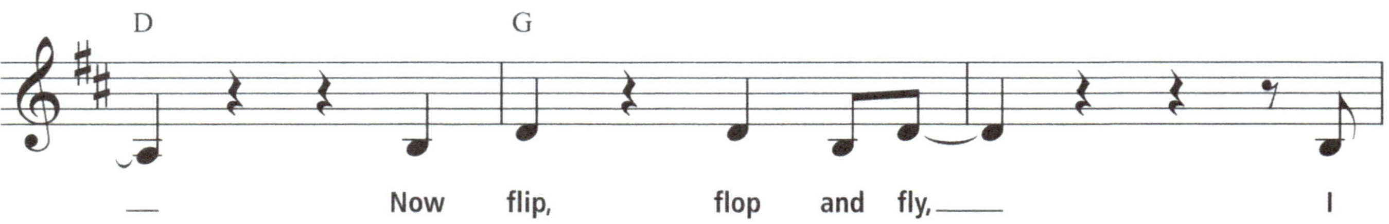

D
G
__ Now flip, flop and fly,____ I

D
A7
don't know the rea - son why.____ Don't ev - er leave me,

G
D
don't ev - er say good - bye.____

Flip, Flop and Fly
Recorder Countermelody

Giant (This Then Is Texas)

(from *Giant*)

Music by Dimitri Tiomkin
Words by Paul Francis Webster

D
Bm
Em7
A7
do
Aus - tin and Hous - ton and A - la - mo, El

D
Bm
Em7
A7
Pa - so, Crys - tal Cit - y, Wa - co.

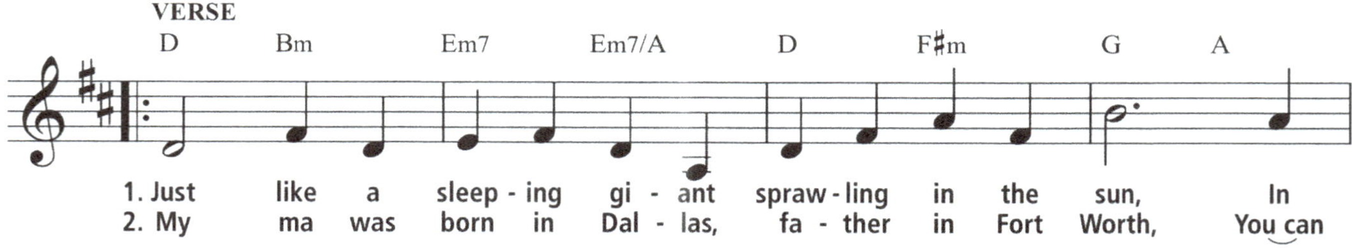

VERSE
D
Bm
Em7
Em7/A
D
F#m
G
A
1. Just like a sleep - ing gi - ant spraw - ling in the sun, In
2. My ma was born in Dal - las, fa - ther in Fort Worth, You can

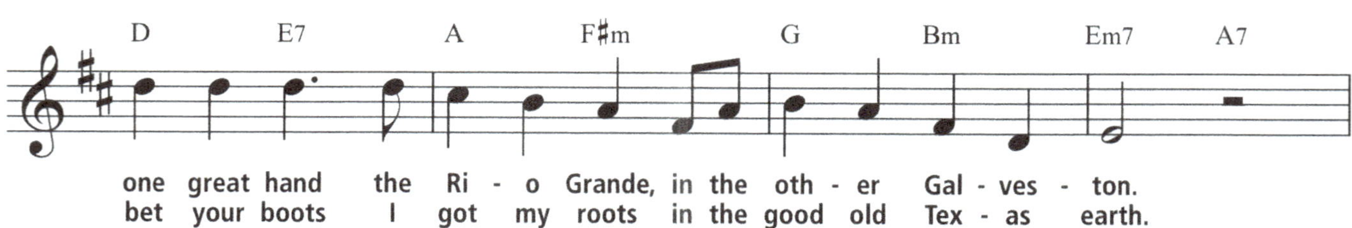

D
E7
A
F#m
G
Bm
Em7
A7
one great hand the Ri - o Grande, in the oth - er Gal - ves - ton.
bet your boots I got my roots in the good old Tex - as earth.

Giant (This Then Is Texas)

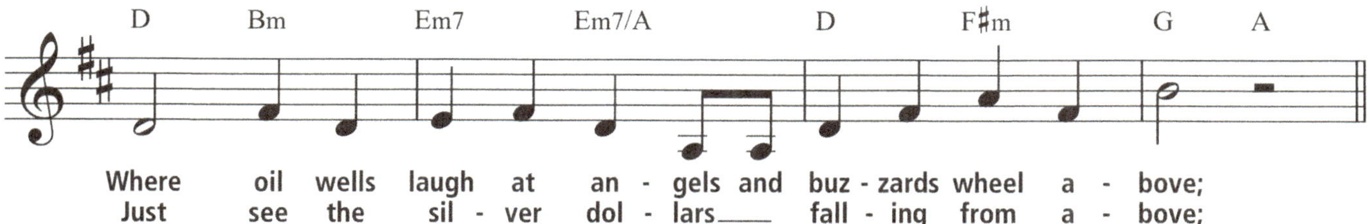

D   Bm   Em7   Em7/A   D   F#m   G   A
Where oil wells laugh at an - gels and buz - zards wheel a - bove;
Just see the sil - ver dol - lars fall - ing from a - bove;

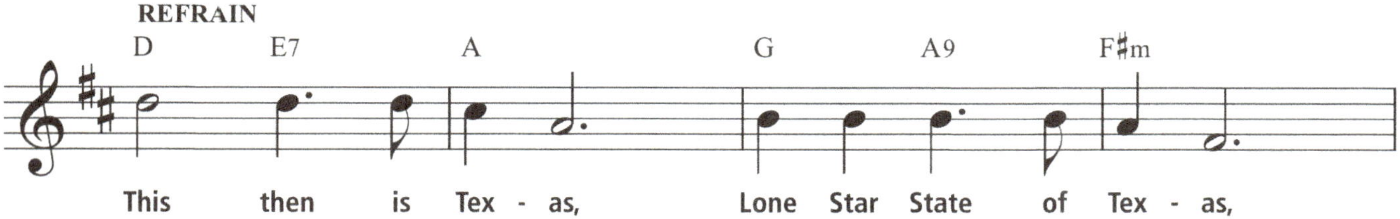

REFRAIN
D   E7   A   G   A9   F#m
This then is Tex - as, Lone Star State of Tex - as,

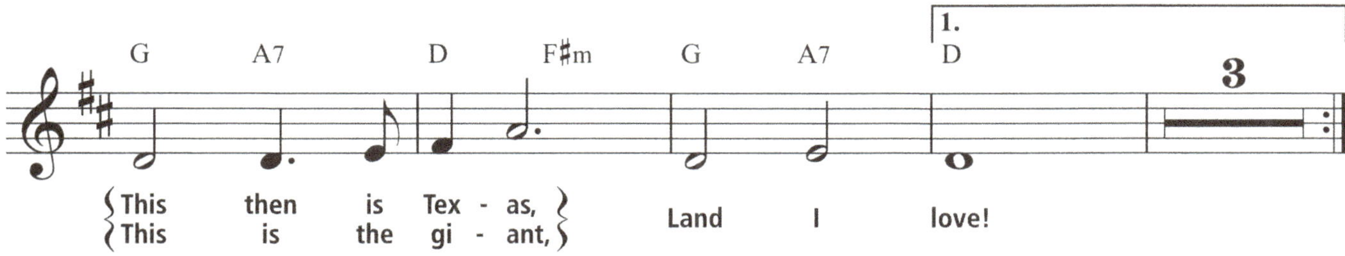

G   A7   D   F#m   G   A7   1. D   3
This then is Tex - as,
This is the gi - ant,
Land I love!

2. D   Em7   A7   D   Em7   A7   D
love! Land I love! Land I love!

A Gift to Share

Words and Music by Rollo A. Dilworth

I have a gift, that's no mys - ter - y. It's the gift of all
gifts, it's the gift to be me. I must share my gift each and
ev - er - y day in the hope that the gifts of the ones a - round
me will come my way. I have a
gift, a gift that is spe - cial.__ It's the gift to be free. I must
share it__ ev - er - y day in hope that the
gifts of the ones a - round me will come my way.

A Gift to Share

Gm7   D7   Gm7   D7   Gm7
I'll shout it high,   I'll shout it low   that   I must share this
I'll   shout it. Yes, I'll   shout   that   I must share this

E♭maj7   Cm7   Dm7   G
gift   I have   ev - 'ry-where   I   go.
gift   I have   ev - 'ry-where   I   go.

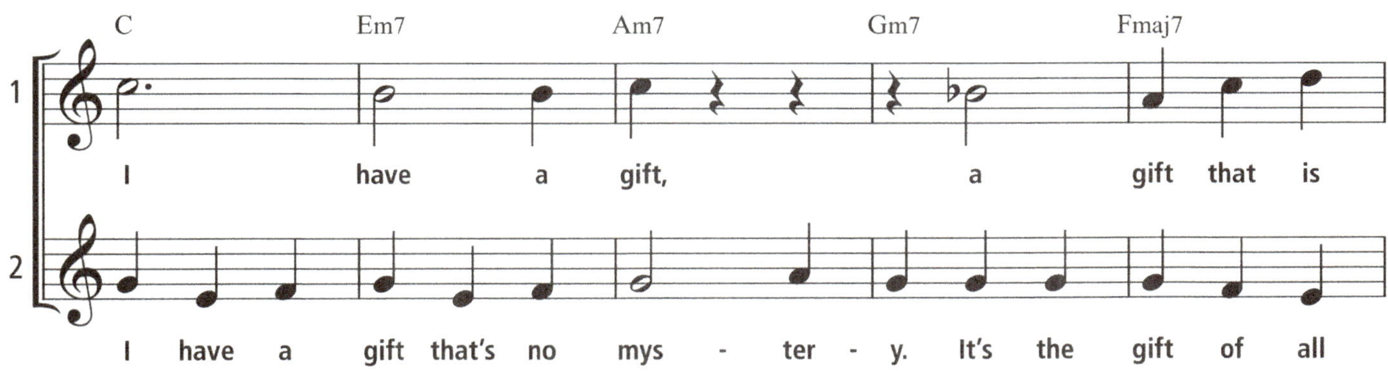

C   Em7   Am7   Gm7   Fmaj7
I   have   a   gift,   a   gift that is
I   have   a   gift that's no   mys - ter - y.   It's the   gift of all

C   D7   C/E   D/F#   G   G7   Am7   Em7
spe-cial,   It's the   gift   to   be   me.   I   must   share it
gifts,   it's the   gift   to   be   me.   I   must   share   my   gift each and

A Gift to Share

ev - er - y day in hope that the gifts of the ones a - round
ev - er - y day in the hope that the gifts of the ones a - round me
me will come my way. I'm a gift.
will come my way. I'm a gift.
I'm a gift. I'm a gift.
I'm a gift. I'm a gift.
I'm a gift.
I'm a gift.

Give a Little Love

Words and Music by Diane Warren and Albert Hammond

REFRAIN
We got to give a lit - tle love, have a lit - tle hope, make
this world a lit - tle bet - ter. Oh - oh whoah,
Oh - oh whoah.
VERSE
1. Liv - ing in this cra - zy world, so caught up in the con - fu - sion.
2. Got the wars on our minds, got the trou - bles on our shoul - ders.
Noth - ing is mak - ing sense for me and you.
Some - times it seems so much what we go through.
May - be we can find a way, there's got to be a so - lu - tion,
May - be if we take the time, time to un - der - stand each oth - er,

Give a Little Love

D   A7   D
How to make a bright - er day, ___   What do ___ we do?
We can learn to make it right. ___   What do ___ we do?
REFRAIN
D   A7   D   A7
We got to give a lit - tle love, have ___ a lit - tle hope, make
D   A7   D
___ this world a lit - tle bet - ter.   Try a lit - tle more, hard -
A7   D   A7
- er than be-fore, let's do what we can do to-geth - er. Oh ___
D   A7   D
whoah - oh, ___ We can ev - en make it bet - ter, yeah. ___
1.
D   A7
Oh whoah, ___ la, la, la, On - ly if we try. ___ ___ We got to ___
(last time repeat refrain ad lib)
2.
D   Bm   Em
___ If ev - 'ry - bod - y took some - bod - y by the hand, ___

Give a Little Love

Bm   Em   A7
May - be ev - 'ry - one___ could learn to love___ and un - der - stand.___
D   A7   D
Oh   whoah, ___   We can real - ly make it   bet - ter,   yeah.___
D   A7   D   A7
2nd time to Refrain
Oh   whoah, ___ la, la, la,   On - ly if we   try.___ (We got to)

Glory, Glory, Hallelujah

Traditional Gospel Song

do
F
(Optional chords)
F7
REFRAIN Glo - ry, glo - ry, hal - le - lu - jah!
1. I feel bet - ter, so much bet - ter,
2. Feel like shout - in' "Hal - le - lu - jah!"
F7
B♭
F
(B♭ - F)
Since I laid my bur - den down.
F
(A7) (Dm7) (A7)
Glo - ry, glo - ry, hal - le - lu - jah!
I feel bet - ter, so much bet - ter,
Feel like shout - in' "Hal - le - lu - jah!"
F
(Dm7) (B♭) (F/C)
C7
(B♭/C) (C7)
F
(B♭ - F)
Repeat Refrain after each verse
Since I laid my bur - den down.

Good King Wenceslas

Traditional

1. Good King Wen - ces - las looked out   On the Feast of Ste - phen,
2. "Hith - er, page, and stand by me,   If thou know'st it, tell - ing,
3. "Bring me flesh and bring me wine,   Bring me pine - logs hith - er,
4. "Sire, the night is dark - er now,   And the wind blows strong - er;

When the snow lay round a - bout,   Deep and crisp and e - ven;
Yon - der pea - sant, who is he?   Where and what his dwell - ing?"
Thou and I will see him dine,   When we bear them thith - er."
Fails my heart, I know not how,   I can go no long - er."

Bright - ly shone the moon that night,   Though the frost was cru - el,
"Sire, he lives a good league hence,   Un - der - neath the moun - tain;
Page and mon - arch forth they went,   Forth they went to - geth - er;
"Mark my foot - steps, good my page!   Tread thou in them bold - ly;

When a poor man came in sight,   Gath'ring win - ter fu - el.
Right a - gainst the for - est fence,   By Saint Ag - nes' foun - tain."
Through the rude wind's wild la - ment,   And the bit - ter weath - er.
Thou shalt find the win - ter's rage   Freeze thy blood less cold - ly."

5. In his master' steps he trod, Where the snow lay dinted;
Heat was in the very sod Which the saint had printed.
Therefore, Christian folk, be sure, Wealth or rank possessing;
Ye who now will bless the poor, Shall yourselves find blessing.

Hava nagila

Jewish Folk Song

Ha - va na - gi - la, ha - va na - gi - la, ha - va na - gi - la,
v' - nis - m'-cha.
v' - nis - m'-cha.
Ha - va n' - ra - n' - na,
ha - va n' - ra - n' - na, ha - va n' - ra - n' - na, v' - nis - m'-cha.
v' - nis - m'-cha. U - ru, u - ru a - chim,
u - ru a - chim b' - lev sa - me - ach, u - ru a - chim b' - lev sa - me - ach,
u - ru a - chim b' - lev sa - me - ach, u - ru a - chim b' - lev sa - me - ach,
u - ru a - chim, u - ru a - chim, b' lev sa - me - ach.

Hava nagila

Recorder Countermelody

Hernando's Hideaway

(from *The Pajama Game*)

Words and Music by
Richard Adler and Jerry Ross
Arranged by Andy Beck

I know a dark se - clud - ed place, a
All you see are sil - hou - ettes, and
place where no one knows your face, where two can share a
all you hear are cas - ta - nets and no one cares a how

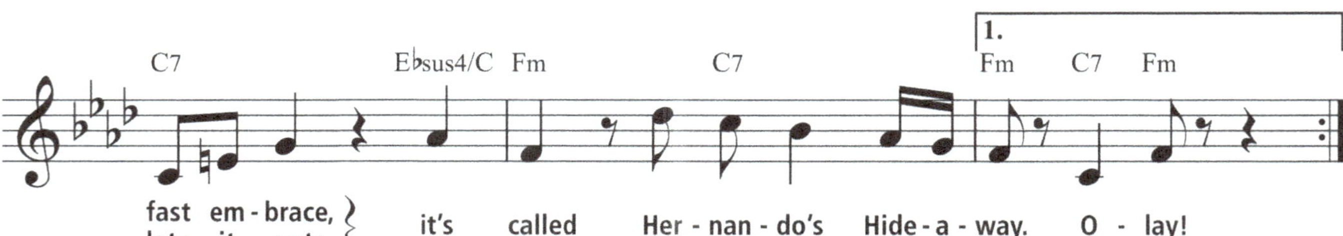
fast em - brace,
late it gets,
it's called Her - nan - do's Hide - a - way. O - lay!
1.
Fm   C7   Fm

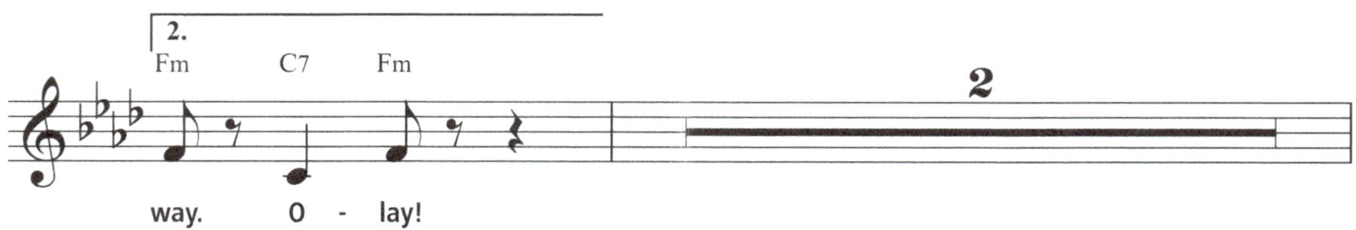
2.
Fm   C7   Fm
way.   O - lay!
2

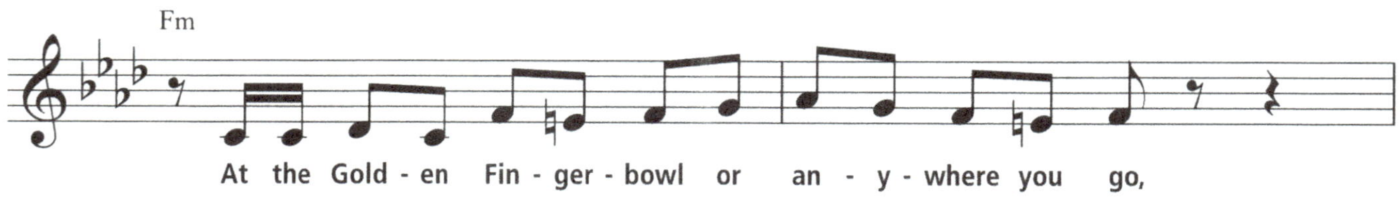
At the Gold - en Fin - ger - bowl or an - y - where you go,

Hernando's Hideaway

you will meet your Un - cle Max and ev - 'ry - one you know.

But if you go to the spot that I am think-ing of,

you will be free to gaze at me and talk of

love! Just knock three times and whis-per low, that

you and I were sent by Joe, then strike a match and

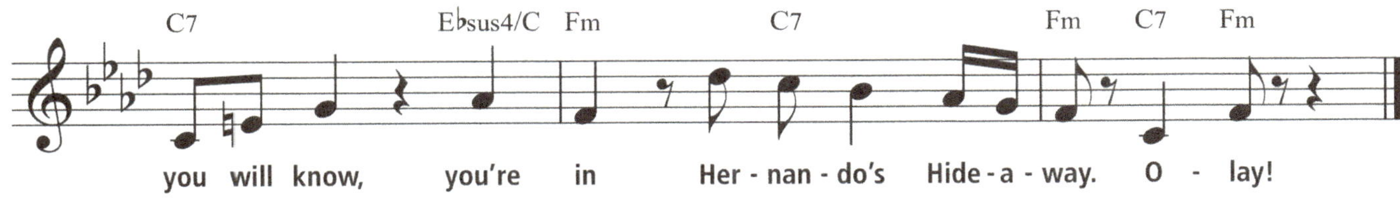

you will know, you're in Her - nan - do's Hide - a - way. O - lay!

Hey, Ho! Nobody Home

Old English Round

do
Em D C Bm7
Hey, ho, no - bod - y home,
Em D C Bm7
Meat nor drink nor mon - ey have I none.
Em D C Bm7
Yet I will be mer - ry, ver - y mer - ry.
Em D C Bm7
Hey, ho, no - bod - y home.
Ostinato 1
Hey, ho, Hey, ho,— I said,
Ostinato 2
Hey, ho, Hey, ho.
Ostinato 3
Hey, ho, Hey, ho.

Hit Me with a Hot Note and Watch Me Bounce

Words and Music by Duke Ellington and Don George

1. Hit me with a hot note and watch me bounce,
2. Hit me with a hot note and watch me burn,
3. Hit me with a hot note and watch me bounce,

Hit me with a hot note and watch me bounce, When
Slap me down with rhy - thm from stem to stern, When
Knock me out with mu - sic in great a - mounts, Oh,

trum - pets heat up, Gim - me a rug to beat up,
sax - es flare up, How can I keep my hair up?
let that beat wave, We're gon - na have a heat wave,

1., 2. 2nd time to next strain   3.   Fine

Hit me with a hot note and watch me bounce.
Hit me with a hot note and watch me bounce.
Hit me with a hot note and watch me bounce.

Hit Me with a Hot Note and Watch Me Bounce

Solo
B♭m
E♭7   A♭maj7
Start that trom - bone slid - in', _____ While I gath - er steam, _
Cm7
F   B♭7   B♭dim   B♭7   D.C al Fine
Keep that tem - po rid - in' _____ And I'll _ come in _ right on _ the beam.

Hooray for Hollywood

Music by Richard A. Whiting
Words by Johnny Mercer
Arranged by Andy Beck

Show-biz fanfare ♩ = c. 132–138
F
mf F
G♭/F
1. do
Hol - ly - wood!
mf
2. do
Hol - ly - wood!
Hol - ly - wood!
G♭/F
Gm7
rit.
C7
Hol - ly - wood!
Hoo - ray for Hol - ly -
Hoo - ray for Hol - ly -

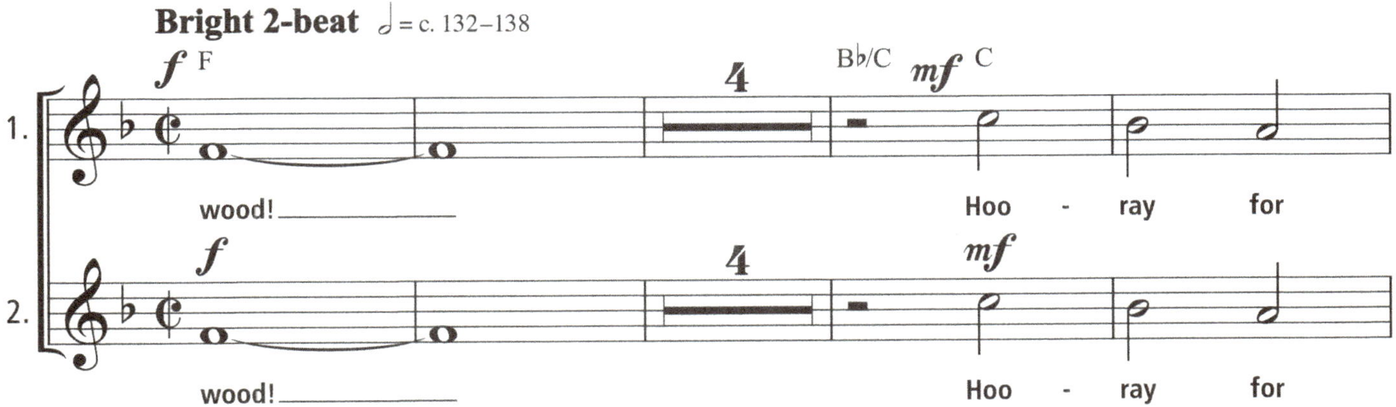

Bright 2-beat ♩ = c. 132–138
f F
B♭/C mf C
1.
wood!
Hoo - ray for
f
2.
wood!
Hoo - ray for

Hooray for Hollywood

F6
F
1.
Hol - ly - wood! ___ That screw - y bal - ly - hoo - ey
2.
Hol - ly - wood! ___ That screw - y bal - ly - hoo - ey

A7
Em7/A
A
1.
Hol - ly - wood, ___ Where an - y of - fice boy or
2.
Hol - ly - wood, ___ Where an - y of - fice boy or

B♭maj7
Gm7(♭5)
C
Faug
Dm6
1.
young me - chan - ic can be a pan - ic with
2.
young me - chan - ic can be a pan - ic

A
E7/B
A
E/G♯
F♯m
A♭7
1.
just a good look - ing pan. ___
2.
And

Hooray for Hollywood

C/E
C#dim7
1.
2.
an - y bar____ maid can be a star____ made,

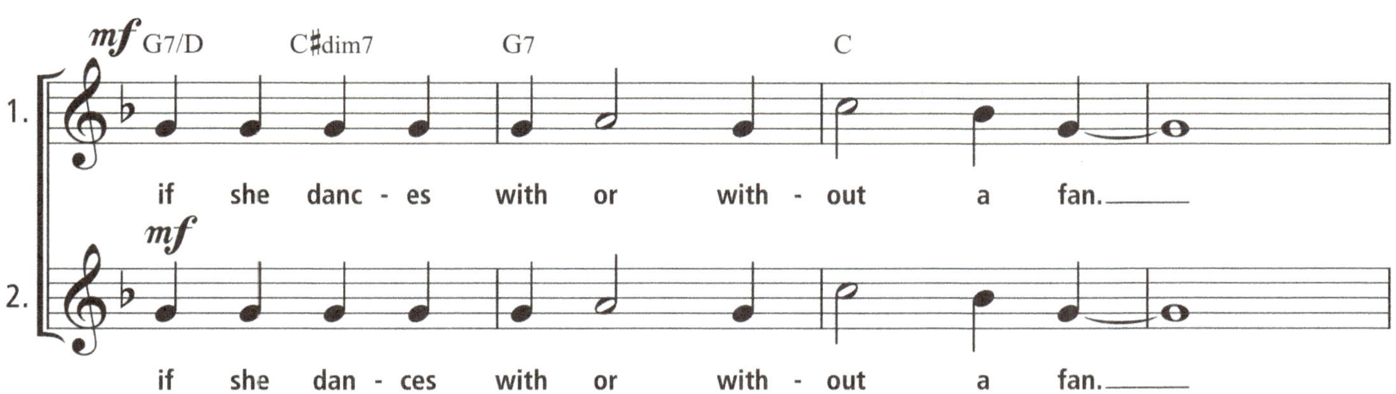

mf G7/D   C#dim7   G7   C
1.
if she danc - es with or with - out a fan.____
mf
2.
if she dan - ces with or with - out a fan.____

Bb/C   F6
1.
Hol - ly -
2.
Hoo - ray for Hol - ly - wood!____

F6   A7   Em7
1.
wood!____   Hol - ly -
2.
Where you're ter - rif - ic if you're e - ven good,____

Hooray for Hollywood

A7
Bbmaj7
Bb9
1. wood! Shir - ley Tem - ple to
2. Where an - y - one at all from Shir - ley Tem - ple to

Gm7(b5)
F
F7/Eb
1. Ai - mee Sem - ple is e - qual - ly un - der -
2. Ai - mee Sem - ple

D7
Gm7
Gm7(b5)
1. stood. Go out and try your luck, You might be
2. un - der - stood. Go out and try your luck, You might be

F
D9
Gm7
C/G
1. Don - ald Duck! Hoo - ray
2. Don - ald Duck! Hoo -

Hooray for Hollywood

C7   C6   C7(b9)   F6
1.   — for Hol - ly - wood!
2.   ray for Hol - ly - wood!

Bb/C   mp F   F6   grad. cresc.
1.   Hol - ly - wood,
mp   grad. cresc.
2.   Hol - ly - wood,

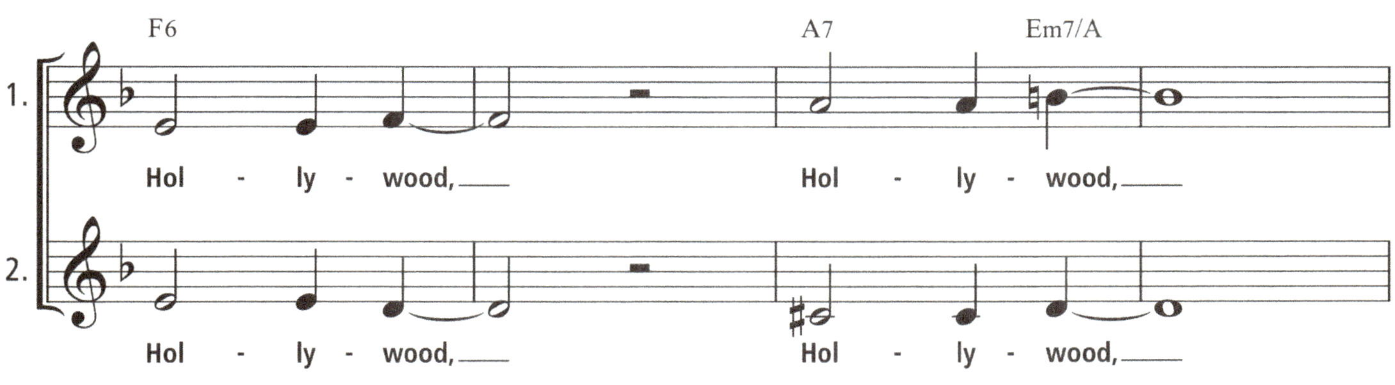

F6   A7   Em7/A
1.   Hol - ly - wood,   Hol - ly - wood,
2.   Hol - ly - wood,   Hol - ly - wood,

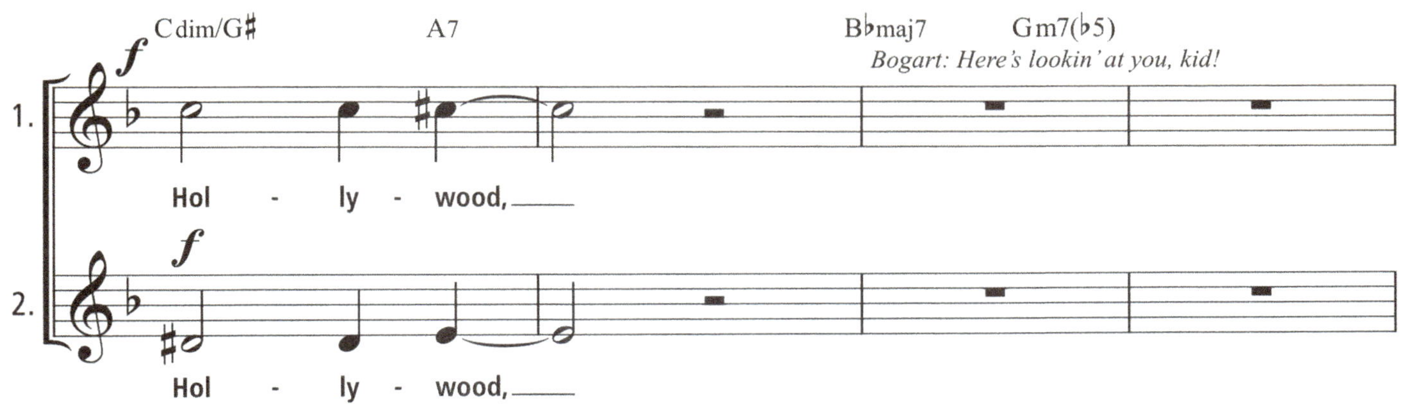

Cdim/G#   A7   Bbmaj7   Gm7(b5)
Bogart: Here's lookin' at you, kid!
1.   Hol - ly - wood,
f
2.   Hol - ly - wood,

Hooray for Hollywood

C6   Dm6   A   E7/B   A   F#m
Swanson: Alright, Mr. DeMille, I'm ready for my close-up.   SCHWARZENEGGER: I'll be bahck!
1.
2.

mf Ab7/Eb   C/E   C#dim7
1.
And   an - y - bar____ maid   can   be   a   star____ made,
2.

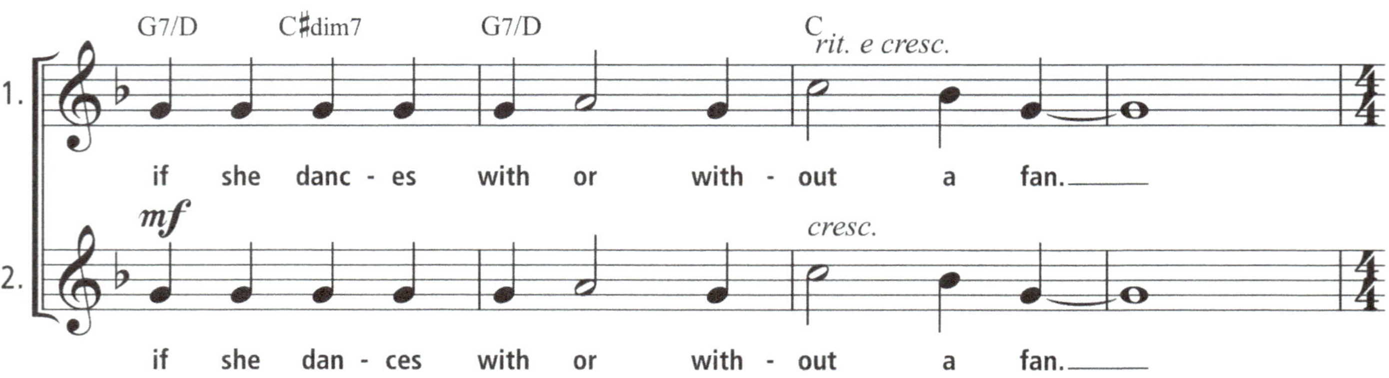

G7/D   C#dim7   G7/D   C
rit. e cresc.
1.
if   she   danc - es   with   or   with - out   a   fan.____
mf   cresc.
2.
if   she   dan - ces   with   or   with - out   a   fan.____

Kick-line ♩ = c. 84
C   f   F   3
1.
Hoo - ray   for   Hol - ly - wood! _
f   3
2.
Hoo - ray   for   Hol - ly - wood! _

Hooray for Hollywood

F6
A7
Em7
You may be home - ly in your neigh - bor - hood, __
You may be home - ly in your neigh - bor - hood, __

A tempo ♩ = c. 132–138
A
B♭maj7
B♭9
But if you think that you can be an ac - tor, see
But if you think that you can be an ac - tor, see

Gm9(♭5)
Gm7
Gm7(♭5)
F
F7/E♭
Mis - ter Fac - tor, he'd make a mon - key look
Mis - ter Fac - tor,

D7
Gm7
Gm7(♭5)
good. With - in a half an hour you'll look like
mon - key look good. With - in a half an hour you'll look like

Hooray for Hollywood

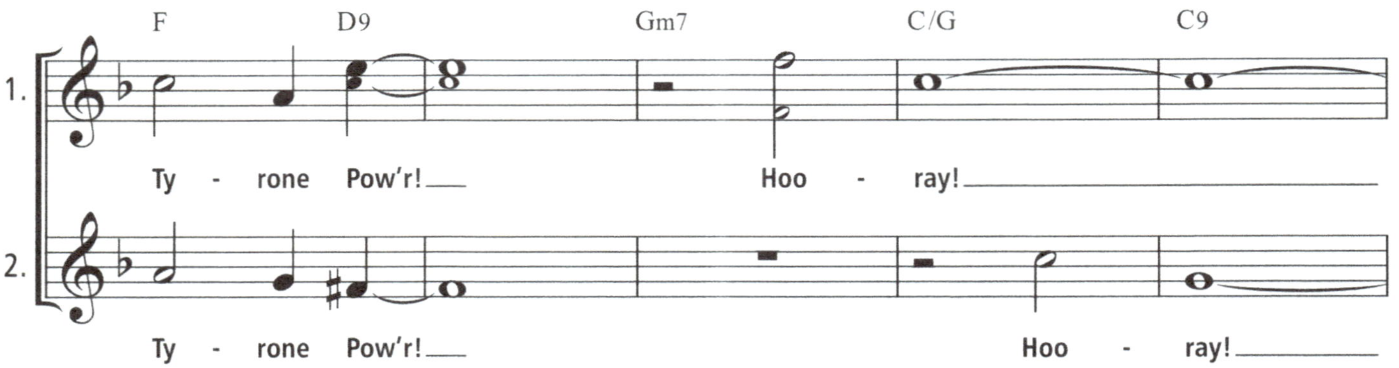

F   D9   Gm7   C/G   C9
1.
Ty - rone Pow'r!___   Hoo - ray!___________________
2.
Ty - rone Pow'r!___   Hoo - ray!___

C9   F/A   D7
1.
___   Hoo - ray!___________________
2.
___   Hoo - ray!___________

Gm7   C/G   C9   C7
1.
Hoo - ray!___________   for Hol - ly -
2.
Hoo - ray!   for Hol - ly -

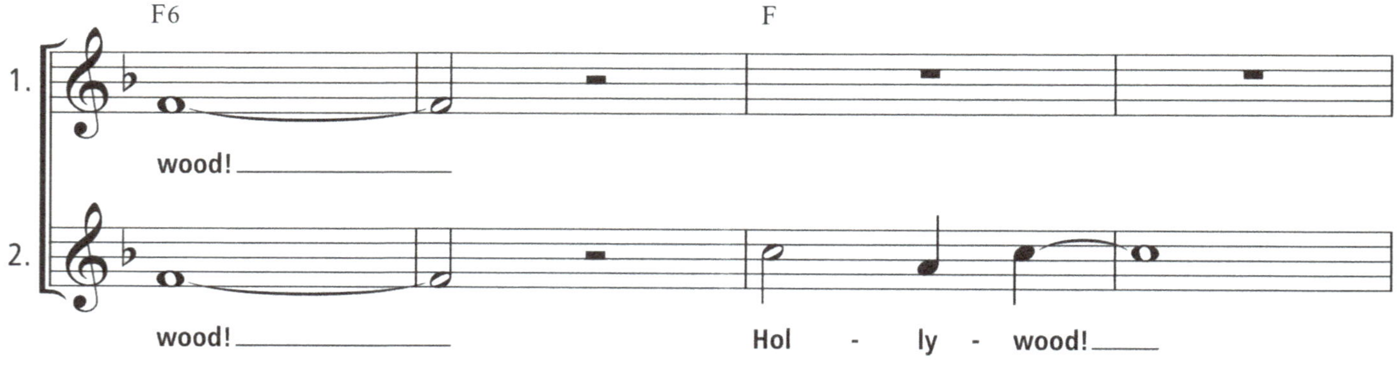

F6   F
1.
wood!___________
2.
wood!___________   Hol - ly - wood!___

Hooray for Hollywood

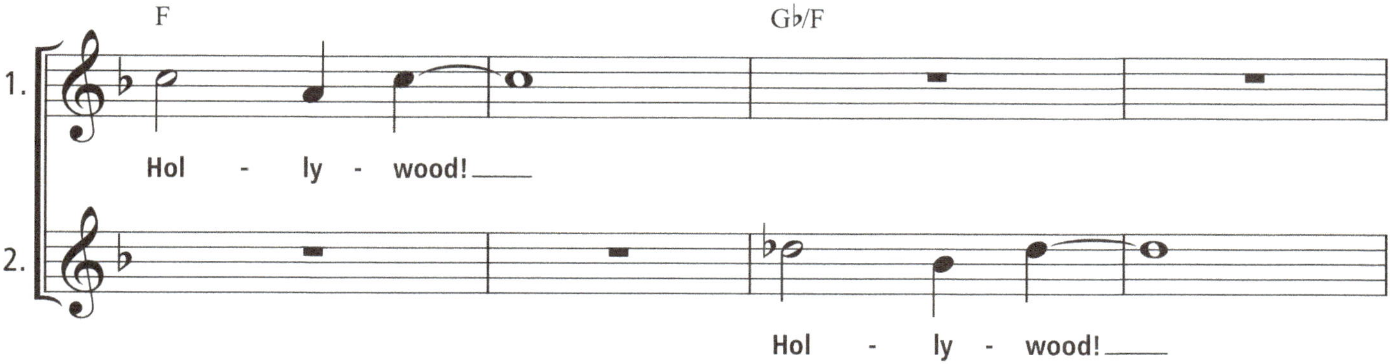

F
G♭/F
Hol - ly - wood! ____
Hol - ly - wood! ____

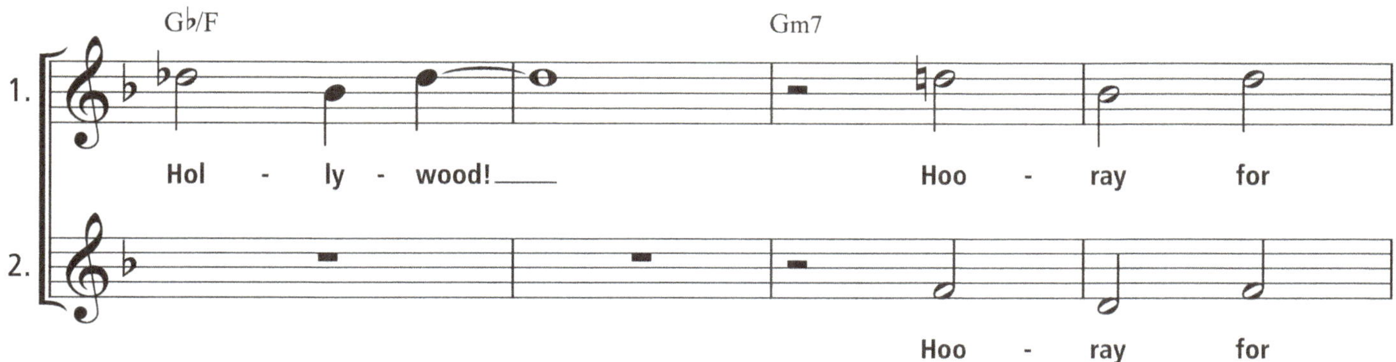

G♭/F
Gm7
Hol - ly - wood! ____
Hoo - ray for
Hoo - ray for

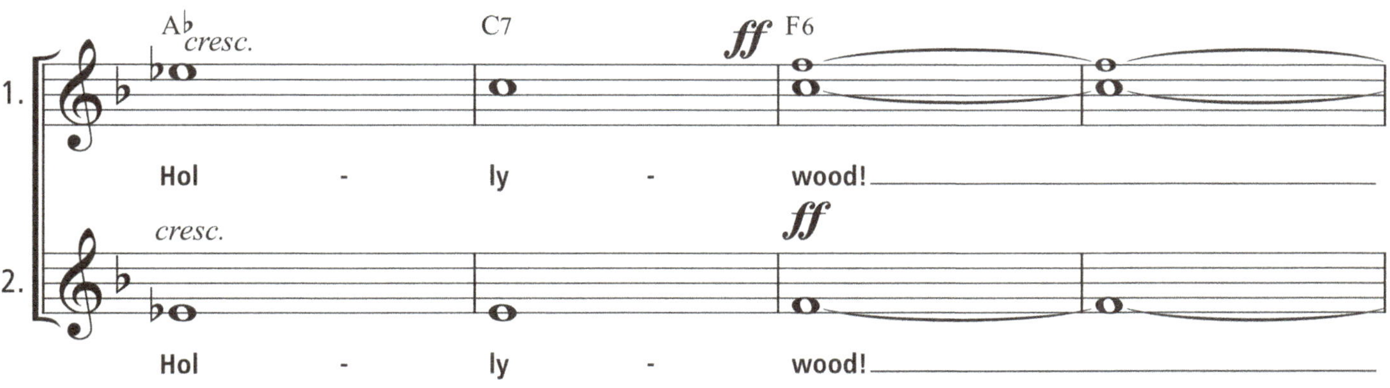

A♭
cresc.
C7
ff
F6
Hol - ly - wood! ____
cresc.
ff
Hol - ly - wood! ____

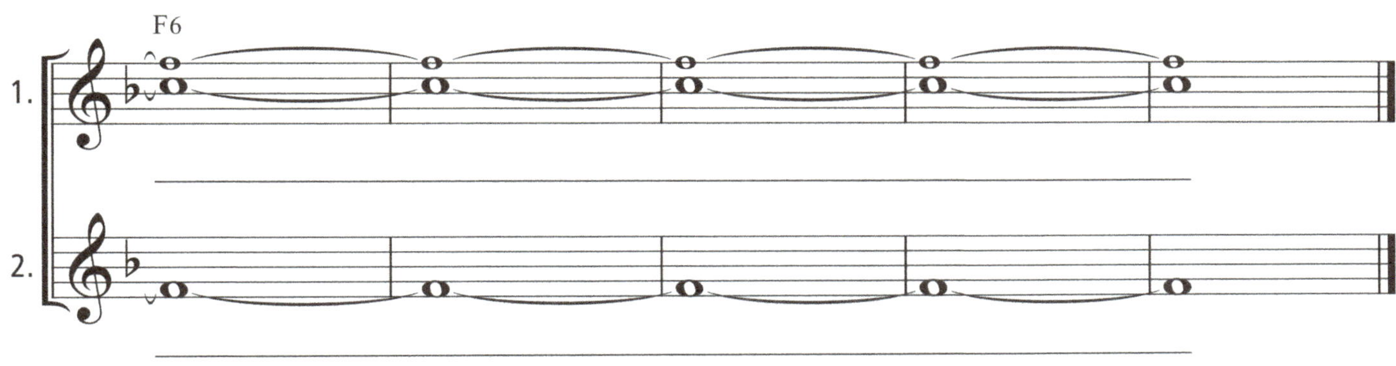

F6

Music by Andy Beck
Words by Andy Beck and Brian Fisher

Hot Chocolate!

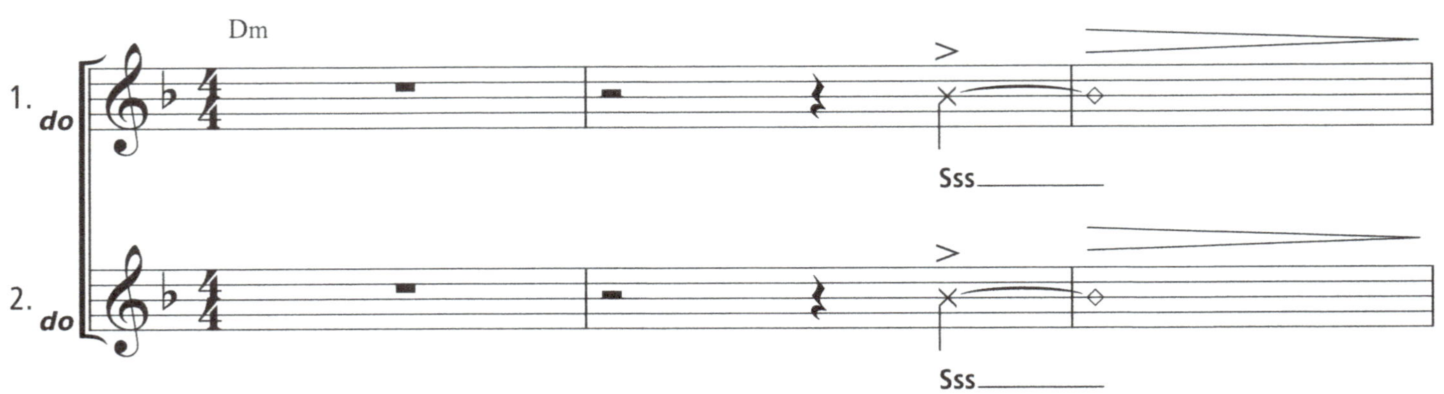

do
do
Dm
Sss
Sss

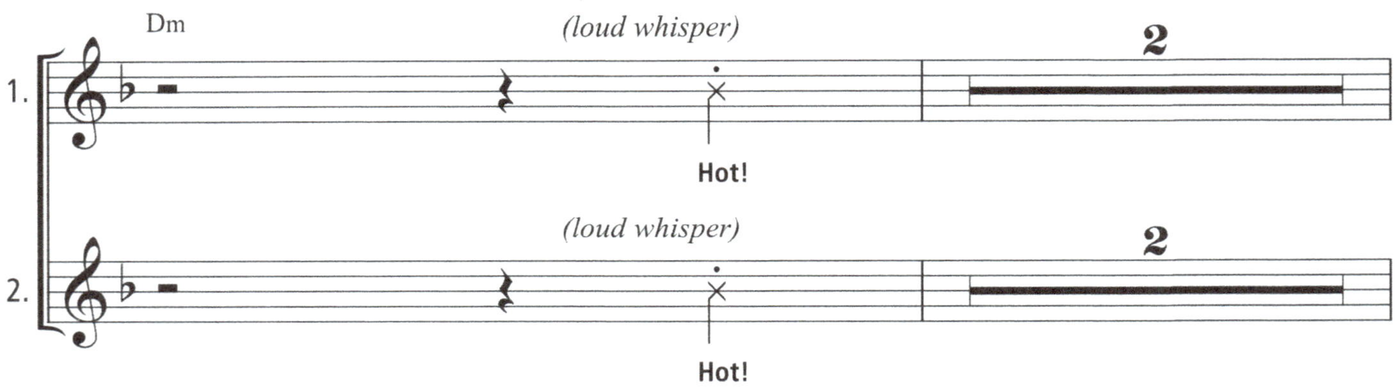

Dm
(loud whisper)
2
Hot!
(loud whisper)
2
Hot!

Dm
A7
mf
Hot, hot, hot, hot choc - 'late,   I can't get e -
mf
Hot, hot, hot, hot choc - 'late,   I can't get e -

Hot Chocolate!

Dm
A7
1. nough.
Hot, hot, hot, hot choc - 'late,
2. nough.
Hot, hot, hot, hot choc - 'late,
A7
Dm
1. It's my fav - 'rite stuff!
mp
2. It's my fav - 'rite stuff!
When the weath - er is
A7/E
Dm
2. freez - ing and you think you'll turn to ice,
Dm
mp
A7/E
1. there is noth - ing more pleas - ing than a mug of par - a -

Hot Chocolate!

dise.
Turn up the heat, make it steam-y and sweet, with
Turn up the heat, make it steam-y and sweet, with
marsh-mal-lows on the top. Come fill me up to the
marsh-mal-lows on the top. Come fill me up to the
top of my cup, I'm gon-na drink ev-'ry drop!
top of my cup, I'm gon-na drink ev-'ry drop!
Hot, hot, hot, hot choc-'late, I can't get e-
Hot, hot, hot, hot choc-'late, I can't get e-

Hot Chocolate!

nough.   Hot, hot, hot, hot choc - 'late,
nough.   Hot, hot, hot, hot choc - 'late,
It's my fav - 'rite stuff!   Hot, hot choc - 'late.
It's my fav - 'rite stuff!
Hot, hot choc - 'late.   Hot, hot choc - 'late.
Sss   Make it steam - y.
Hot, hot choc - 'late.   Hot, hot
Sss   Rich and cream - y.   Sss
(approx. one third of choir)
Marsh - mal - lows are float - ing on the

Hot Chocolate!

D5
cresc.
1. choc - 'late.   Hot,   hot   choc - 'late.
cresc.
2. Make it steam - y.   Sss   Rich and cream - y.
cresc.   (rejoin section)
3. top.   Whipped cream.   I'm nev - er gon - na stop.

Gm7   Fmaj7   Edim7
f
1. Turn   up __ the heat, make it   steam - y __ and sweet,   with marsh-mal - lows on   the
f
2. Turn   up __ the heat, make it   steam - y __ and sweet,   with marsh-mal - lows on   the

Dm   Gm7   Fmaj7
1. top.   Come   fill __ me up   to the   top   of __ my cup,
2. top.   Come   fill __ me up   to the   top   of __ my cup,

Hot Chocolate!

I'm gon - na drink ev - 'ry drop!
I'm gon - na drink ev - 'ry drop!
Hot, hot choc - 'late, hot choc - 'late, I can't get e -
Hot, hot, hot, hot choc - 'late, I can't get e -
Hot, hot, hot, hot choc - 'late, I can't get e -
nough. Hot, hot choc - 'late, hot choc - 'late,
nough. Hot, hot, hot, hot choc - 'late,
nough. Hot, hot, hot, hot choc - 'late,
DESCANT
(rejoin section)

Hot Chocolate!

A7
Dm
A7
It's my fav - 'rite stuff!
I can't get e -
It's my fav - 'rite stuff!
I can't get e -

Dm
A
Faug/A
mp
f
nough!
I need a fix made from scratch or a mix. Hot
mp
f
nough!
I need a fix made from scratch or a mix. Hot

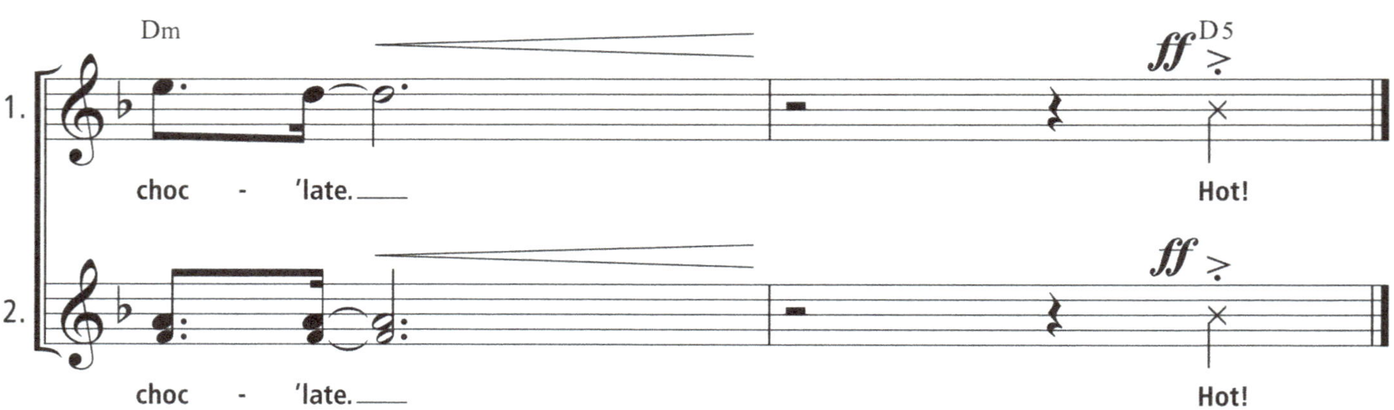
Dm
ff
D5
choc - 'late.
Hot!
ff
choc - 'late.
Hot!

96

I Bought Me a Cat

American Folk Song
Arranged, with new words, by Sally K. Albrecht

With a bounce ♩ = c. 92
mf
C
do—
I bought me a cat, my cat pleased me. I fed my cat un-der
C   Fmaj7   G7   mf   Dm7   G   cymbal claps 3x   fists on waist   C
1. Cat goes *fid - dle - i - fee.
2. yon - der tree. Cat goes fid - dle - i - fee.
C   G   C
I bought me a hen, my hen pleased me. I
C   Fmaj7 G7   C
fed my hen un - der yon - der tree. Hen goes chim - my chuck, chim - my chuck.
Dm7   G cymbal claps 3x   fists on waist   C
1. Cat goes fid - dle - i - fee.
mf
2. Cat goes fid - dle - i - fee.

* Pronounced: *fih-duhl-eye-fee.*

I Bought Me a Cat

C G7 C
1. I bought me a duck, my duck pleased me. I fed my duck un-der
2. I bought me a duck, my duck pleased me. I fed my duck un-der
mel.

C Fmaj7 G7   C   Am
1. yon-der tree.   Hen goes chim-my chuck, chim-my chuck.
2. yon-der tree. Duck goes quack, quack.

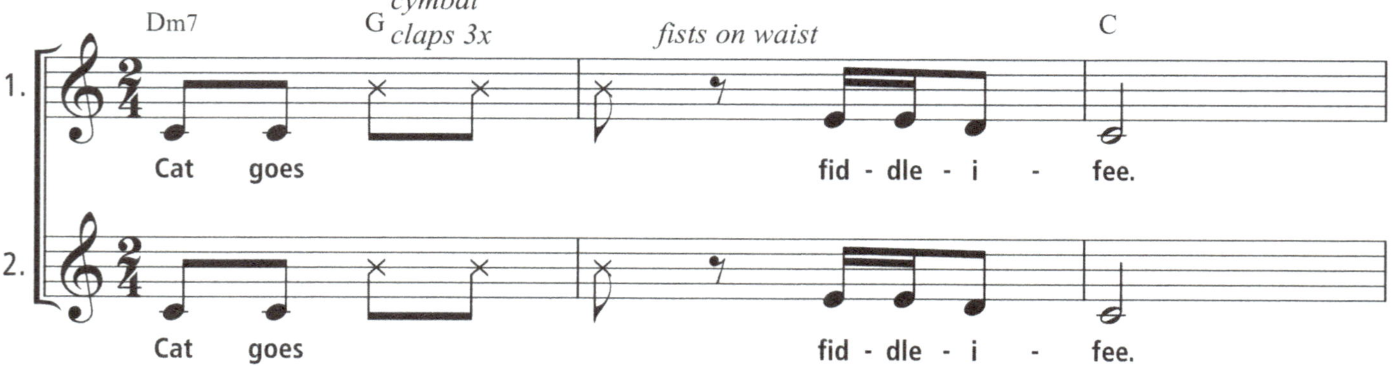

Dm7   cymbal G claps 3x   fists on waist   C
1. Cat goes   fid-dle-i-fee.
2. Cat goes   fid-dle-i-fee.

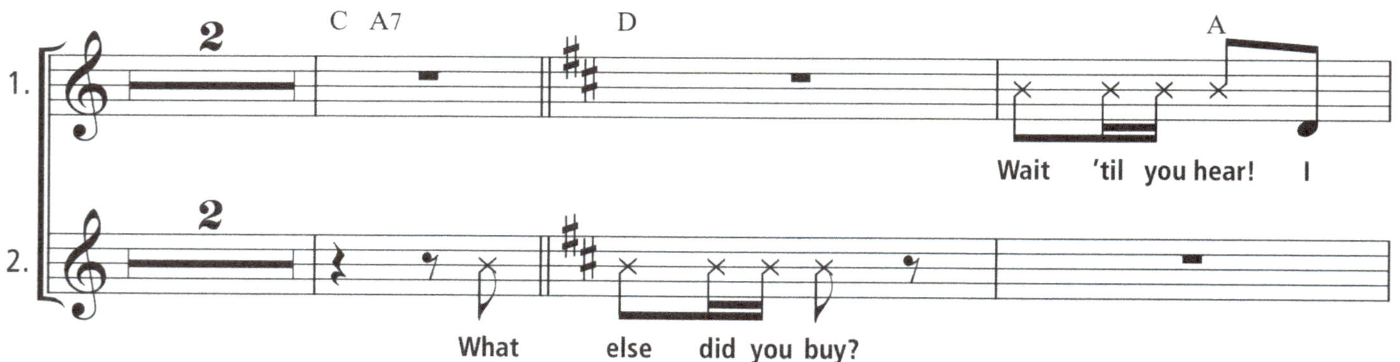

C A7   D   A
1. Wait 'til you hear! I
2. What else did you buy?

I Bought Me a Cat

bought me a goose, my goose pleased me. I fed my goose un-der
Bought me a goose. I fed my goose un-der
yon-der tree. Goose goes his-sy, his-sy.
yon-der tree. Duck goes quack, quack.
Hen goes chim-my chuck, chim-my chuck. Cat goes fid-dle-i-
Cat goes fid-dle-i-
fee. I bought me a
fee. I bought me a pig, my

I Bought Me a Cat

sheep, my sheep pleased me. I fed my sheep un-der yon-der tree.
pig pleased me. I fed my pig un-der yon-der tree.

Sheep goes baa, baa. Goose goes his-sy, his-sy.
Pig goes grif-fy, grif-fy.

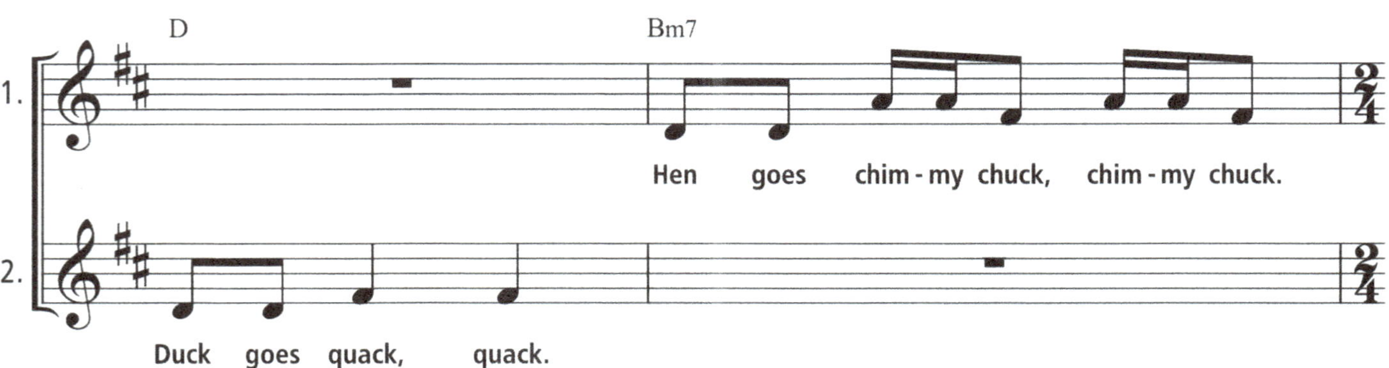

Hen goes chim-my chuck, chim-my chuck.
Duck goes quack, quack.

cymbal claps 3x fists on waist
Cat goes fid-dle-i-fee.
Cat goes fid-dle-i-fee.

I Bought Me a Cat

SPOKEN SOLO:
But wait! There's more!

I bought me a horse,
I bought me a dog.
I

and they pleased me. We fed them all un-der
bought me a cow, and they pleased me. We fed them all un-der

yon - der tree. Horse goes neigh, neigh.
yon - der tree. Dog goes bow - wow, bow - wow.

Sheep goes baa, baa.
Cow goes moo, moo. Pig goes grif - fy, grif - fy.

I Bought Me a Cat

Eb
Cm
2/4
Goose goes his - sy, his - sy.
Hen goes chim-my chuck, chim-my chuck.
2/4
Duck goes quack, quack.

Fm7
cymbal
Bb
claps 3x   fists on waist
Eb
rit.
mp
2/4
Cat goes   fid-dle-i - fee.   I
mp
2/4
Cat goes   fid-dle-i - fee.   I

Freely, in four ♪ = c. 96

Eb
mime handing over money
make kissing sounds
got   me a wife,   my wife pleased me.   We
got   me a wife,   my wife pleased me.   We

Eb
Bb7
Eb
3/4
had   a   pic - nic un - der   yon - der   tree.   My   wife said, "Hon - ey, hon - ey,
3/4
had   a   pic - nic un - der   yon - der   tree.   My   wife said, "Hon - ey, hon - ey,

I Bought Me a Cat

Tempo I ♩ = c. 92

Eb   Cm7   Abmaj7   Bb7   Eb
rit. e cresc.
2
1. no more buy - ing an - i - mals, please!"
cresc.
2
2. no more buy - ing an - i - mals, please!"

Eb
1. If you came a - long, then you could hear the
2. If you came a - long, thne you could hear the

Eb   Abmaj7   Bb7
1. man and wife say - ing, "Oh, my dear." Be -
2. man and wife say - ing, "Oh, my dear." Be -

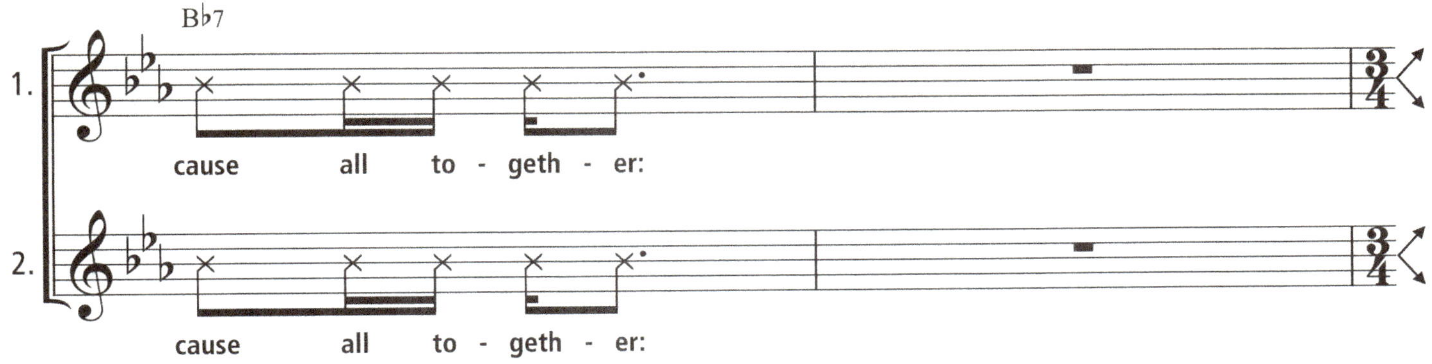

Bb7
1. cause all to - geth - er:
2. cause all to - geth - er:

I Bought Me a Cat

(Divide into 8 equal groups, enter by number. Keep repeating and building to end.)

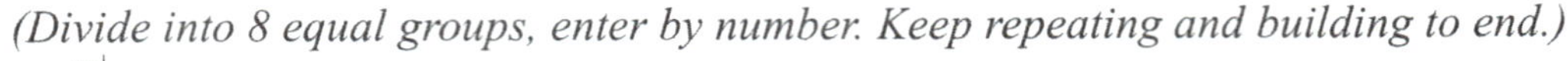

GROUP 4
GROUP 2
2. Horse goes neigh, neigh
GROUP 3
GROUP 1
1. Dog goes bow - wow, bow - wow   bow - wow, bow - wow,
4. Sheep goes baa, baa,
neigh, neigh, neigh, neigh,
3. Cow goes moo, moo, moo, moo,
bow - wow, bow - wow, bow - wow, bow - wow,

I Bought Me a Cat

GROUP 6
6. Goose goes his - sy, his - sy,
GROUP 4
baa, baa, baa, baa,
GROUP 2
neigh, neigh, neigh, neigh,
GROUP 7
GROUP 8
GROUP 3
moo, moo, moo, moo,
GROUP 5
5. Pig goes grif - fy, grif - fy, grif - fy, grif - fy,
GROUP 1
bow - wow, bow - wow, bow - wow, bow - wow,

I Bought Me a Cat

his - sy, his - sy, his - sy, his - sy,
baa, baa, baa, baa,
neigh, neigh, neigh, neigh,
8. Hen goes chim - my chuck, chim - my chuck,
7. Duck goes quack, quack, quack, quack,
moo, moo, moo, moo,
grif - fy, grif - fy, grif - fy, grif - fy,
bow - wow, bow - wow, bow - wow, bow - wow,

I Bought Me a Cat

SPOKEN DUET
(man/wife) or SOLO:
All right, already!
That's enough!

Eb
stomp 2x
stomp 2x
his - sy, his - sy, his - sy, his - sy,
baa, baa, baa, baa,
neigh, neigh, neigh, neigh,
chim-my chuck, chim-my chuck, chim-my chuck, chim-my chuck,
quack, quack, quack, quack,
moo, moo, moo, moo,
grif - fy, grif - fy, grif - fy, grif - fy,
bow - wow, bow - wow bow - wow, bow - wow,

I Bought Me a Cat

GROUPS 4 and 6
Cat goes fid - dle - i,
GROUPS 2 and 8
Cat goes fid - dle - i,
GROUPS 3 and 7
Cat goes fid - dle - i,
GROUPS 1 and 5
Cat goes fid - dle - i,
stomp 2x
cat goes fid - dle - i - fee!
cat goes fid - dle - i - fee!
cat goes fid - dle - i - fee!
cat goes fid - dle - i - fee!
cymbal claps 3x
fists on waist

I Got Rhythm

Music and Lyrics by
George Gershwin and Ira Gershwin

I got rhy - thm,
I got dai - sies
I got mu - sic,
In green pas - tures,
I got my man, Who could ask for an - y-thing more?
Old Man Trou - ble, I don't mind him, You won't
find him 'Round my door, I got star - light,
I got sweet dreams, I got my man, who could
ask for an - y-thing more, Who could ask for an - y-thing more?

I Shall Sing

Words and Music by Van Morrison

It's Possible (McElligot's Pool)
(from *Seussical the Musical*)

Music by Stephen Flaherty
Lyrics by Lynn Ahrens and Dr. Seuss
Arranged by Andy Beck

This might be a pool, like I've read of in books, con-
nect-ed to one of those un-der-ground brooks! An un-der-ground riv - er that
starts here and flows right un-der the bath - tub! And then, who knows? It's
pos - si - ble.
An - y-thing's pos - si - ble!
It might go a - long down where no one can see, right
un-der State High - way Two - Hun-dred-and - Three! Right un-der the wag - ons? Right

It's Possible (McElligot's Pool)

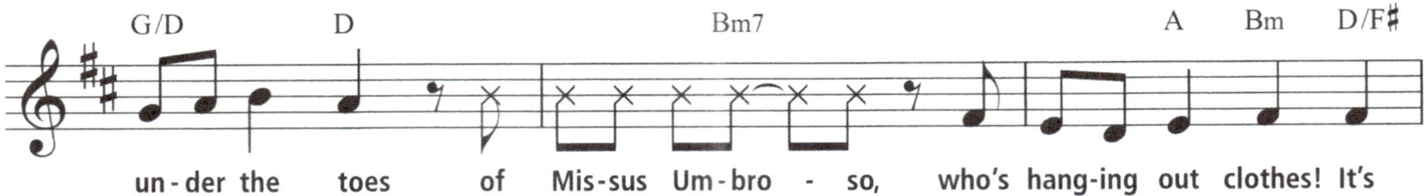

G/D   D   Bm7   A   Bm   D/F#
un - der the   toes   of   Mis - sus Um - bro - so,   who's hang - ing out clothes! It's

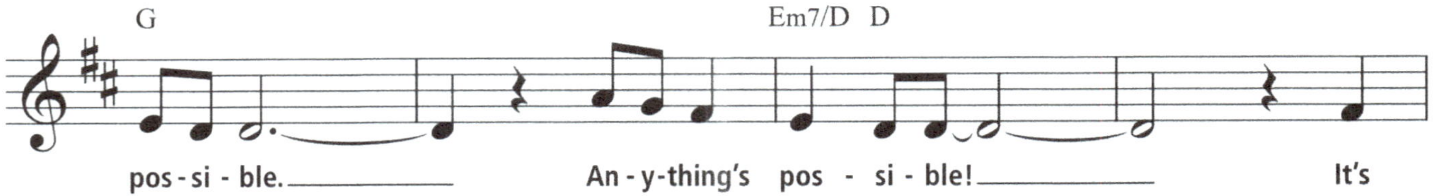

G   Em7/D D
pos - si - ble.______   An - y - thing's pos - si - ble!______   It's

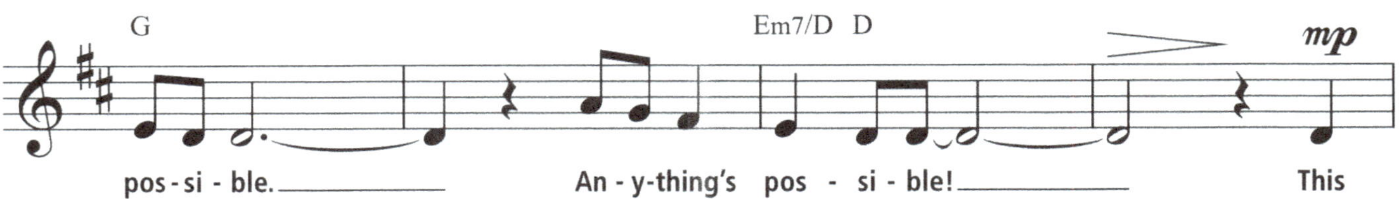

G   Em7/D D   mp
pos - si - ble.______   An - y - thing's pos - si - ble!______   This

G9   D/F#
might be a riv - er, now might-n't it be,   con - nect-ing Mc - El - li-got's pool

Bm7   G9
grad. cresc.
__ with the   sea!   Then may-be some fish__ might   be swim-ming,   swim-ming to - ward

A   Asus4   D/A   A   f   D
__ me!______   Oh, the sea is so full__ of a

It's Possible (McElligot's Pool)

G/D   D   Bm7   A   A/C#   D
num-ber of fish. If a fel-low is pa - tient, he might get his wish! And

D   G/D   D   Bm7   A
that's why I think_ that I'm not such a fool when I sit here and fish in Mc-

A   Bm   D/F#   G   mf   Em7/D   D
El - li-got's pool. It's pos-si-ble._ An - y-thing's pos - si - ble!_

D   G
_ It's pos - si - ble._ An - y-thing's

Em7/D   D   molto rit.   D/F#   G
pos - si - ble!_ It's pos - si - ble.

G   f   slowly, with conviction   Em7/D   D
An - y-thing's pos - si - ble!_

Ja-Da

Words and Music by Bob Carleton
Arranged by Susan Brumfield

Swing style
Fmaj7   D7   G7   C7   Fmaj7   Gm7
1. do
Ja-Da,   Ja-Da,   Ja - Da, Ja - Da, jing, jing, jing.
2. do
Ja-Da,   Ja-Da,   Ja - Da, Ja - Da, jing, jing, jing.
3. do
Ja-Da,   Ja-Da,   Ja - Da, Ja - Da, jing, jing, jing.

Fmaj7   D7   G7   Gm   C7
1.
Ja-Da,   Ja-Da,   Ja - Da, Ja - Da, jing, jing, jing.
2.
Ja-Da,   Ja-Da,   Ja - Da, Ja - Da, jing, jing, jing.
3.
Ja-Da,   Ja-Da,   Ja - Da, Ja - Da, jing, jing, jing.

Ja-Da

Fmaj7
A♭dim7
Gm7
C7
1.
That's a fun-ny lit-tle bit of mel-o-dy.
2.
Lit - tle mel-o-dy;
3.
Swing - in' mel-o-dy;

Fmaj7
A♭dim7
Gm7
C7
1.
It's so sooth-ing and ap - peal-ing to me. It goes
2.
add some har - mo-ny.
3.
mel - o - dy and har - mo-ny.

Fmaj7
D7
G7
C7
Fmaj7
1.
Ja - Da, Ja - Da, Ja - Da, Ja - Da, jing, jing, jing.
2.
Ja - Da, Ja - Da, Ja - Da, Ja - Da, jing, jing, jing.
3.
Ja - Da, Ja - Da, Ja - Da, Ja - Da, jing, jing, jing.

Jambo Bwana
(Hello, Sir)

Traditional Swahili Phrases
Words and Music by
Ruth Morris Gray

Moderato, with excitement ♩ = c. 92
G Am/E G C G/D
1. do Jam - bo, jam - bo bwana, jam - bo___ jam - bo.
2. do Jam - bo, jam - bo bwana, jam - bo,___ jam - bo.

G Am/E G Am/C G
1. Jam - bo jam - bo bwana, jam - bo,___ jam - bo.
2. Jam - bo, jam - bo bwana, jam - bo,___ jam - bo.

G Am/E G C G/D G
1. Jam - bo, jam - bo bwana, jam - bo,___ jam - bo.
2. Jam - bo, jam - bo bwana, jam - bo,___ jam - bo.

Jambo Bwana

Jam - bo, jam - bo bwa - na, jam - bo,___ jam - bo.
Jam - bo, jam - bo bwa - na, jam - bo,___ jam - bo.

Solo
Ha - ba - ri ga - ni ra - fi - ki?
Jam - bo, jam - bo.
Jam - bo, jam - bo.

How are you do - ing to - day, my friend?
Jam - bo,___ jam - bo.
Jam - bo,___ jam - bo.

Jambo Bwana

Solo 2
G   mf   D7   G   D
A - san - te   n - zu - ri   sa - na.

1.
Jam - bo,   jam - bo.

2.
Jam - bo,   jam - bo.

G   D7   G   (end solo) G   Am/C   C/D   G
I thank you, I'm ver - y fine.

1.
1.
Jam - bo,___ jam - bo.

2.
Jam - bo,___ jam - bo.

2.
G   Am/C   C/D G   C (mf)   D   G   G/D   D
Jam - bo,___ jam-bo.   Ha-ku - na ma-ta - ta.   Jam - bo, jam - bo.

(mf)
Jam - bo,___ jam-bo.   Ha-ku - na ma-ta - ta.   Jam - bo, jam - bo.

Jambo Bwana

C   D   G   G/D   D
1. No wor - ries, no prob - lems here.   Jam - bo, jam - bo.
2. No wor - ries, no prob - lems here.   Jam - bo, jam - bo.

C   D   G   G/D   D
1. Ha - ku - na ma - ta - ta.   Jam - bo, jam - bo.
2. Ha - ku - na ma - ta - ta.   Jam - bo, jam - bo.

C   D   G   Am/C   C/D G
1. No wor - ries, no prob - lems here.   Jam - bo,___ jam - bo.
2. No wor - ries, no prob - lems here.   Jam - bo,___ jam - bo.

Jambo Bwana

Optional: poco a poco accelerando (2nd time)
Solo 3 or Small Group (second time only)
p–f
O jam - bo.
Jam - bo, jam - bo bwa - na, jam - bo,___ jam - bo.
p–f
Jam - bo, jam - bo bwa - na, jam - bo,___ jam - bo.
O jam - bo,___ jam - bo.
Jam - bo, jam - bo bwa - na, jam - bo,___ jam - bo.
Jam - bo, jam - bo bwa - na, jam - bo,___ jam - bo.
O jam - bo. O jam - bo,___
Jam - bo, jam - bo bwa - na, jam - bo,___ jam - bo.
Jam - bo, jam - bo bwa - na, jam - bo,___ jam - bo.

Jambo Bwana

Just a Snap-Happy Blues

Words and Music by Norma Jean Luckey

Dee bah doo___ bop a dop, Dee bah doo___
bop a dop, Dee bah doo___ bah dee bah dah bah doo bah___
Doo bah doo bah doo wah___ dool'-ya doo bah dee bah,
doo bah doo bah___ dee doo bah doo bah doo wah___
Dah bah doo bah___ bah___ bah dah Dah bah doo bah___ bah___
dop Dah bah doo bah___ bah___ bah dah,

Just a Snap-Happy Blues

Dah bah doo bah___ bah___ dop,   wah   wah
wah da,   Dah bah dah bah dop bah   dah___
Doo   wee   doo bop
Doo   bah doo bah doo wah,___
Dee   doo bah doo bop   Doo   wah   doo bop
Doo   bah doo bah doo wah,
Dee   doo bah doo bop   Doo   wee

Just a Snap-Happy Blues

doo bop,
Dee doo bah doo bop
Doo bah doo bah doo wah, ___

Doo wee doo bop,
Dah bah doo bah ___ bah ___ bah dah
Dah bah doo bah ___ bah ___
Doo bah doo bah doo wah, ___

Dee doo bah doo bop doo wah doo bop
dop, Doo bah doo bah ___ bah ___ bah dah
Doo bah doo bah doo wah,

Just a Snap-Happy Blues

F7
C7
Dee   doo bah doo bop   Doo   wee
Dah bah doo bah___ bah___ dop   Wah   wah

D.C. al Fine
B♭7   F7   C7
doo bop
wah dah   Dah bah dah bah dah bah   dah___
Doo   bah doo bah doo wah___

La borinqueña
(Beloved Island Home)

Music by Felix Astol Artés
Words by Manuel Fernández Juncos
English Words by Kathleen Bernath

La tie - rra de Bo - rin - quen, Don - de he na - ci - do yo,
How beau - ti - ful, Bo - rin - quen, be - lov - ed is - land home.
Es un jar - dín flo - ri - do De má - gi - co pri - mor.
Thy moun - tains and green val - leys, thy sea - shore laced with foam!
Un cie - lo siem - pre ní - ti - do Le sir - ve de do - sel,
Down from the blue and cloud - less sky, sun sheds its ra - dience calm.
Y dan a - rru - llo plá - ci - do Las o - las a sus pies. Cuan - do a sus
Whis - pers the wave a - cross the sand lul - la - bies to the palm. When he dis -
pla - yas vi - no Co - lón, Ex - cla - mó lle - no de ad - mi - ra - ción:
cov - ered thy beau - ty rare, ex - claimed Co - lum - bus, "No land so fair,

La borinqueña

E   3   C#   F#m
do
"Es - ta es la lin - da tie - rra   Que bus - co yo;
Is - land of bright en - chant - ment! I've sought for thee,

B   3   E   B7   3
Es_______ Bo - rin - quen la hi - ja, La hi - ja del mar y el
Daugh - ter of gold - en glo - ry, of flow-ers, of sun and

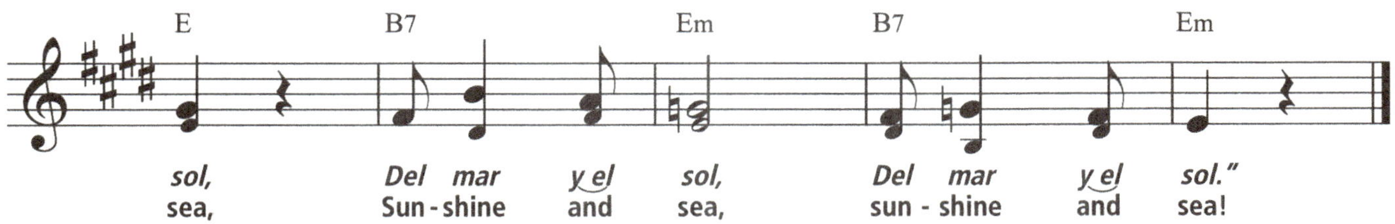

E   B7   Em   B7   Em
sol,   Del mar y el sol,   Del mar   y el sol."
sea,   Sun-shine and sea,   sun-shine and sea!

La golondrina
(The Swallow)

Music by Narciso Serradell
Spanish Words by Martinéz de la Rosa
Based on a French poem by Nicetro de Zamaçois
English Words by Aura Kontra

Guitar: capo 3
¿A - don - de i - rá veloz y fa - ti - ga - da,
Oh, where, oh, where has sum - mer's swal - low flown,
la go - lon - dri - na que de a - quí se va?
So swift in flight, yet wear - y and a - lone?
O si en el vien - to se ha - lla - rá ex - tra - via - da
Oh, should the wind - y skies lead her a - stray,
bus - can - do a - bri - go y no lo en - con - tra - rá.
she'll nev - er find a place where she can stay.
Jun - to a mi le - cho le pon - dré su ni - do,
As I lie sleep - ing she'll re - turn to me safe - ly;

La golondrina

A C D F E G A C
en don - de pue - da la es - ta - ción pa - sar.
Here, she can lin - ger till morn-ing calls her a - way.
A C D F
Tam - bién yo es - toy en la re - gión per - di - do,
I, too, have wan - dered, leav-ing home far be - hind me;
E7 G7 A C E G E7 G7 A C
¡Oh! cie - lo san - to y sin po - der vo - lar.
Since I'm not free, I know I'm here to stay.

La mariposa
(The Butterfly)

Folk Song from Bolivia
English Words by Aura Kontra

La la la la lai la lai la lai la lai lai lai lai lai,
La la la la lai la lai la lai la lai la la la la la lai lai lai.
Al son de las ma - tra - cas to - dos can - tan y bai - lan
Hear the rat - tles' rhyth - mic beat, Call - ing us to sing and dance
La mo - re - na - da. Con las pal - mas, (clap)
to the live - ly sound. Clap your hands now, (clap)
con los ta - cos. (stamp) ¡Vi - va la fies - ta!
kick your heels up, (stamp) turn your part - ner 'round.
¡Vi - va la fies - ta! ¡Vi - va la fies - ta! (clap)
Turn your part - ner 'round, turn your part - ner 'round.

Las mañanitas

Folk Song from Mexico
English Words by Lupe Allegria

Es - tas son las ma - ña - ni - tas Que can -
Hear us sing las ma - ña - ni - tas as the

ta - ba el Rey Da - vid, A las mu - cha - chas bo -
morn - ing light ap - pears, And the gen - tle bird will

ni - tas Se las can - ta - mos a - quí. Des peir - ta, mi bien, des -
join in the hap - py mu - sic he hears. Oh, wake up and see the

pier - ta, Mi - ra que ya a - ma - ne - ció; Ya los
sun - shine. Oh, wake up and meet the day. Hear, the

pa - ja - ri - llos can - tan, La lu - na ya se me - tió.
morn - ing bird is sing - ing, the sil - ver moon has gone a - way.

The Lion Sleeps Tonight

Lyrics and Revised Music by
George David Weiss, Hugo Peretti and Luigi Creatore
Arrangement for Recording by Michael Story
Vocals Arranged by Jeff Funk

Moderate shuffle, swing eighths

Wee wee-um-mum-o-weh.

Wim-o-weh, o-wim-o-weh, o-wim-o-weh, o-wim-o-weh, o-

wim-o-weh, o-wim-o-weh, o-wim-o-weh, o-wim-o-weh, o- wim-o-weh, o-wim-o-weh.

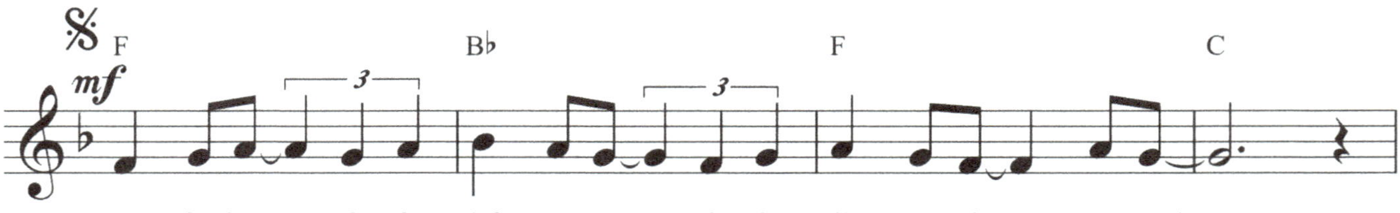
1. In the jun - gle, the might - y jun - gle, the li - on sleeps to - night.
2. Near the vil - lage, the peace - ful vil - lage, the li - on sleeps to - night.
In the jun - gle, the qui - et jun - gle, the li - on sleeps to - night.
Near the vil - lage, the qui - et vil - lage, the li - on sleeps to - night.

The Lion Sleeps Tonight

Wee _______ ooh wee-um - mum - o - weh. _______
Wim-o-weh, o-wim-o-weh, o - wim-o-weh, o-wim-o-weh, o - wim-o-weh, o-wim-o-weh, o -

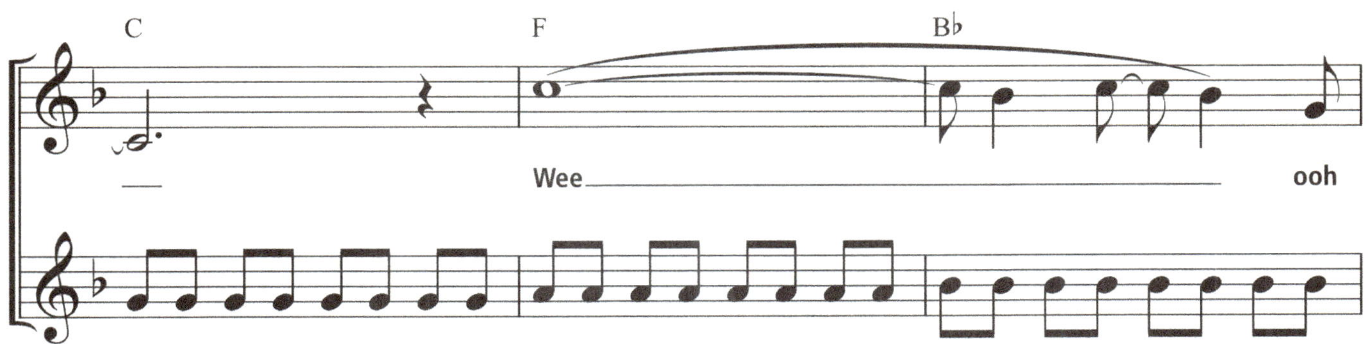

Wee _______ ooh
wim-o-weh, o-wim-o-weh, o - wim-o-weh, o-wim-o-weh, o - wim-o-weh, o-wim-o-weh, o -

To Coda
D.S. al Coda
wee - um - mum - o - weh. _______
wim - o - weh, o - wim - o - weh, o - wim - o - weh, o - wim - o - weh.

133

The Lion Sleeps Tonight

Coda
C   F   B♭
Weh,   weh,
(continue 8 ms.)
wim - o - weh, o - wim - o - weh.

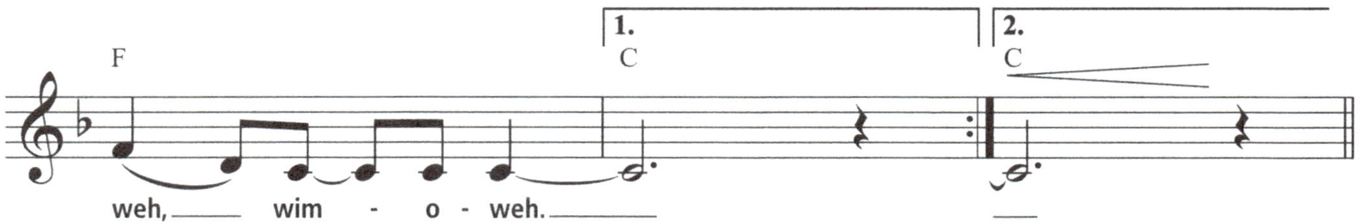

F   1. C   2. C
weh,   wim - o - weh.

F   3   p   B♭   3
3. Hush,   my   dar   -   ling,   don't   fear,   my   dar   -   ling,   the

F   C   mf F   3
li - on   sleeps   to - night.   Hush,   my   dar - ling,   don't

B♭   3   F   C
fear,   my   dar - ling,   the   li - on   sleeps   to - night.

The Lion Sleeps Tonight

Wee ________
ooh wee-um - mum - o - weh. ___
Wim-o-weh, o-wim-o-weh, o - wim-o-weh, o-wim-o-weh, o - wim-o-weh, o-wim-o-weh, o -

Wee ________ ooh
wim-o-weh, o-wim-o-weh, o - wim-o-weh, o-wim-o-weh, o - wim-o-weh, o-wim-o-weh, o -

wee - um - mum - o - weh. ________
(continue to end)
wim - o - weh, o - wim - o - weh, o - wim - o - weh, o - wim - o - weh.

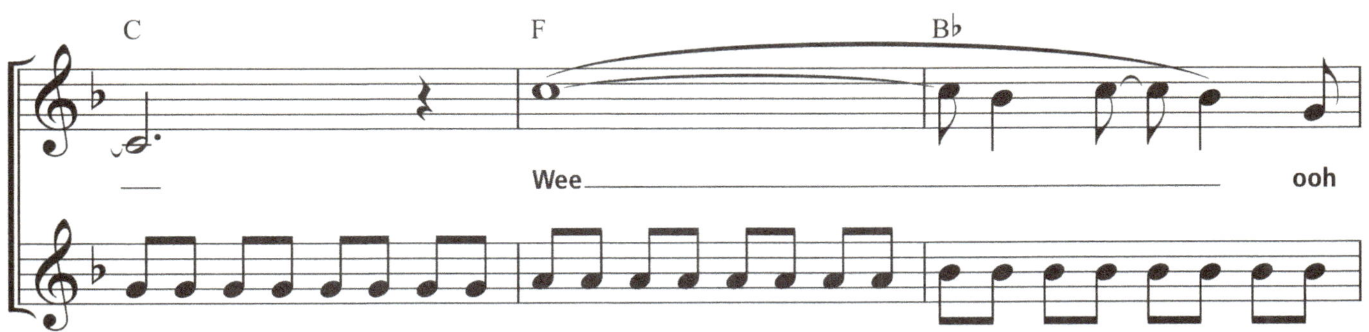

The Lion Sleeps Tonight

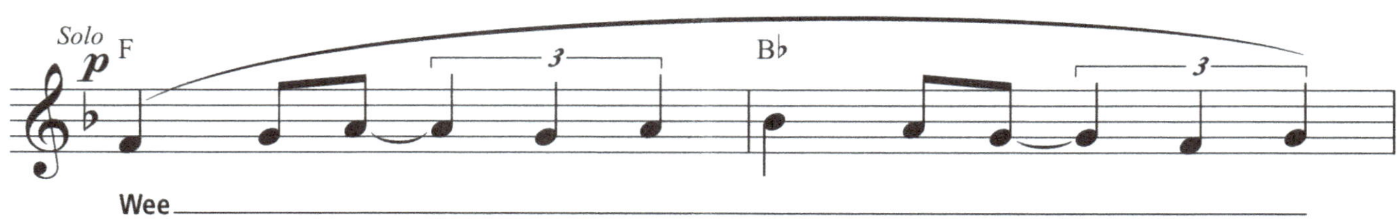

Little Shop of Horrors

Music by Alan Menken
Words by Howard Ashman

Lit - tle shop,_ lit - tle shop-pa hor - rors. Lit - tle shop,_ lit -
- tle shop-pa ter - ror. Call a cop._ Lit - tle shop-pa hor - rors.
No, oh, oh, no - oh!____ Lit - tle shop,_ lit -
- tle shop-pa hor - rors. Bob - sh' - bop,_ lit - tle shop-pa ter - ror.
Watch 'em drop. Lit - tle shop-pa hor - rors. No, oh, oh, no - oh!__
Shing-a - ling, what a creep-y thing to be hap - pen - ing!__ (Look

Little Shop of Horrors

out, look out, look out, look out!) Shang - a - lang, feel the Sturm and Drang in the
air. (Yeah, yeah, yeah.) Sha - la - la,
stop right where you are. Don't move a thing. You bet - ter,
you bet - ter, tell - in' you, you bet - ter tell your ma - ma
some - thin's gon - na get her. She bet - ter,
ev - 'ry - bod - y bet - ter be - ware. (Come-a come-a come-a.)
No, oh, oh, no, oh, oh, no, oh, oh, no!

Loigratong

Folk Song from Thailand
English Words by Alice Firgau

G(I)   C(IV)   G(I)
wan pen___ deup sip song___ nam gau nong tem ta-ling rao tang
The ri - ver is ris - ing, the moon, it is full. Ev - 'ry -
C(IV)   D(V)
lai___ chai ying sa-nook gan - jing wan loi - gra-tong
one___ feels so hap-py and glad on Loi - gra-tong.
G(I)
loi loi - gra-tong loi loi - gra-tong loi - gra -
Loi, Loi - gra-tong, Loi, Loi - gra-tong, Loi - gra -
G(I)   C(V)   D(V)
tong gan lah ow koh___ churn nong kay oh ock ma lum wong lum
tong. Come, float your___ boat, then join the dance with me. We
G(I)   C(IV)
wong wan loi - gra-tong lum wong wan loi - gra-tong boon ja
dance on Loi - gra-tong, we dance on Loi - gra-tong, And we're
G(I) C(IV) G(I) C(IV) G(I) C(IV) G(I)
song hey rao sook jai boon ja song hey rao sook jai
hap - py as can be, and we're hap - py as can be.

Mama Don't 'Low

Folk Song from the United States

do
G
1. Ma-ma don't 'low no gui-tar play-in' 'round here,
2. Ma-ma don't 'low no ban-jo pick-in' 'round here,
G
D7
Ma-ma don't 'low no gui-tar play-in' 'round here,
Ma-ma don't 'low no ban-jo pick-in' 'round here,
G
G7
C
I don't care what Ma-ma don't 'low, Gon-na play my gui-tar an-y-how,
I don't care what Ma-ma don't 'low, Gon-na pick my ban-jo an-y-how,
G
D7
G
Ma-ma don't 'low no gui-tar play-in' 'round here.
Ma-ma don't 'low no ban-jo pick-in' 'round here.

The Marines' Hymn

Traditional

Guitar: capo 3
f with spirit
a
A   E7   A   E7   A
C   G7   C   G7   C
do
From the halls of Mon - te - zu - ma To the shores of Trip-o - li;

a
A   E7   A   E7   A
C   G7   C   G7   C
We fight our coun-try's bat - tles In the air, on land, and sea.

b
D   A   D   A
F   C   F   C
First to fight for right and free - dom And to keep our hon-or clean,

a
A   E7   A   E7   A
C   G7   C   G7   C
We are proud to claim the ti - tle of U - ni-ted States Ma - rine.

Now That's Tap

Words and Music by Ann Duquesnay,
Daryl Waters, and Zane Zacharoff

Give 'em flash, Give 'em style and a great big big big

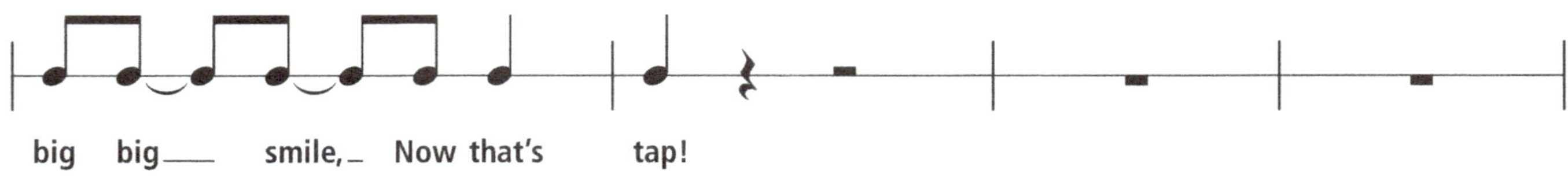
big big smile, Now that's tap!

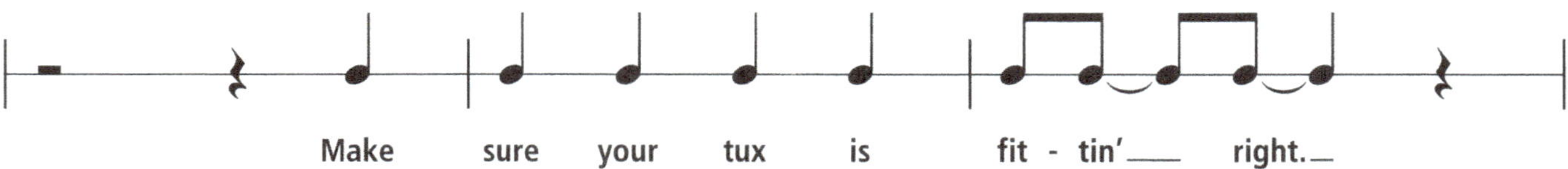
Make sure your tux is fit - tin' right.

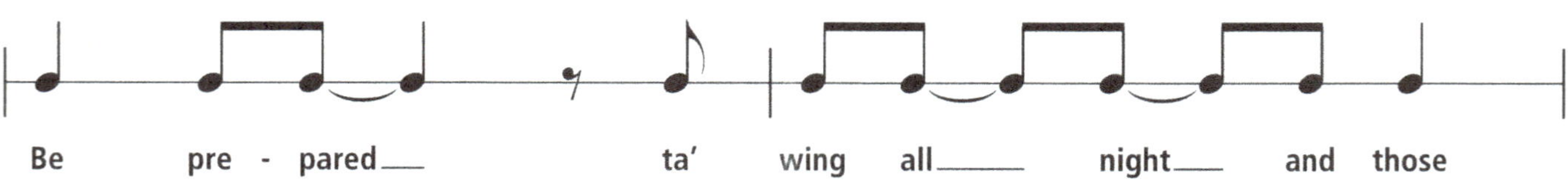
Be pre - pared ta' wing all night and those

pearl - y whites, moon - beam bright, Now that's tap!

Now That's Tap

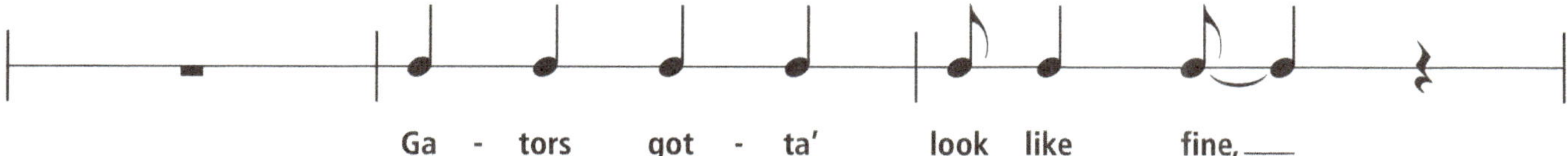

Ga - tors got - ta' look like fine,

Slick your kitch-in' greas - y shine, Tell the world I

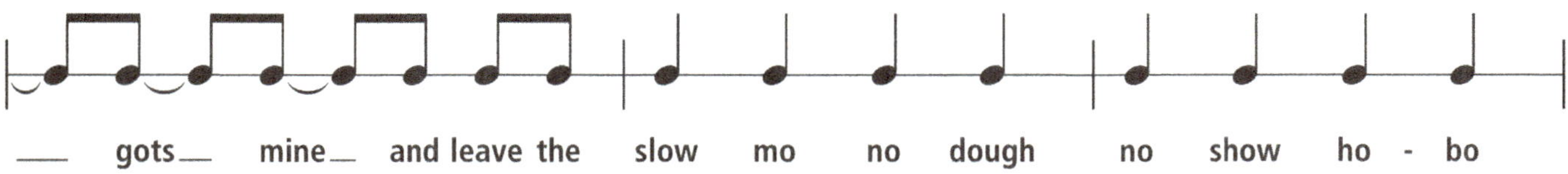

gots mine and leave the slow mo no dough no show ho - bo

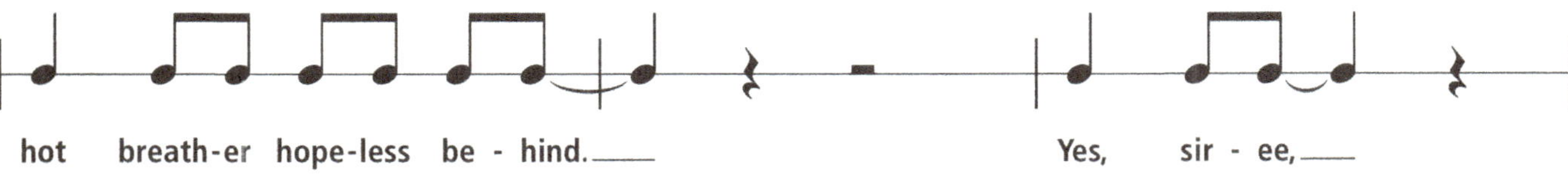

hot breath-er hope-less be - hind. Yes, sir - ee,

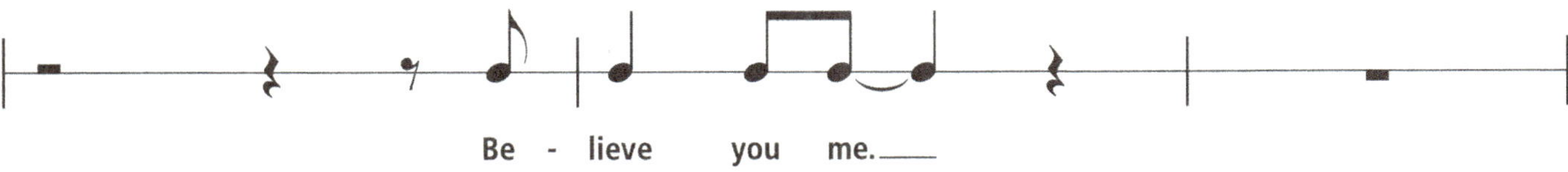

Be - lieve you me.

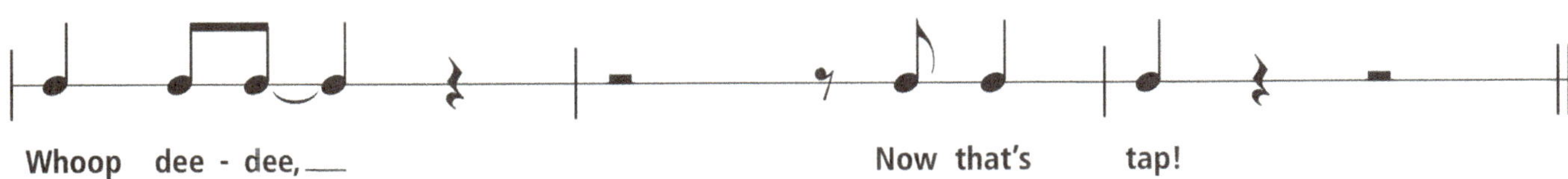

Whoop dee - dee, Now that's tap!

Now That's Tap

Percussion

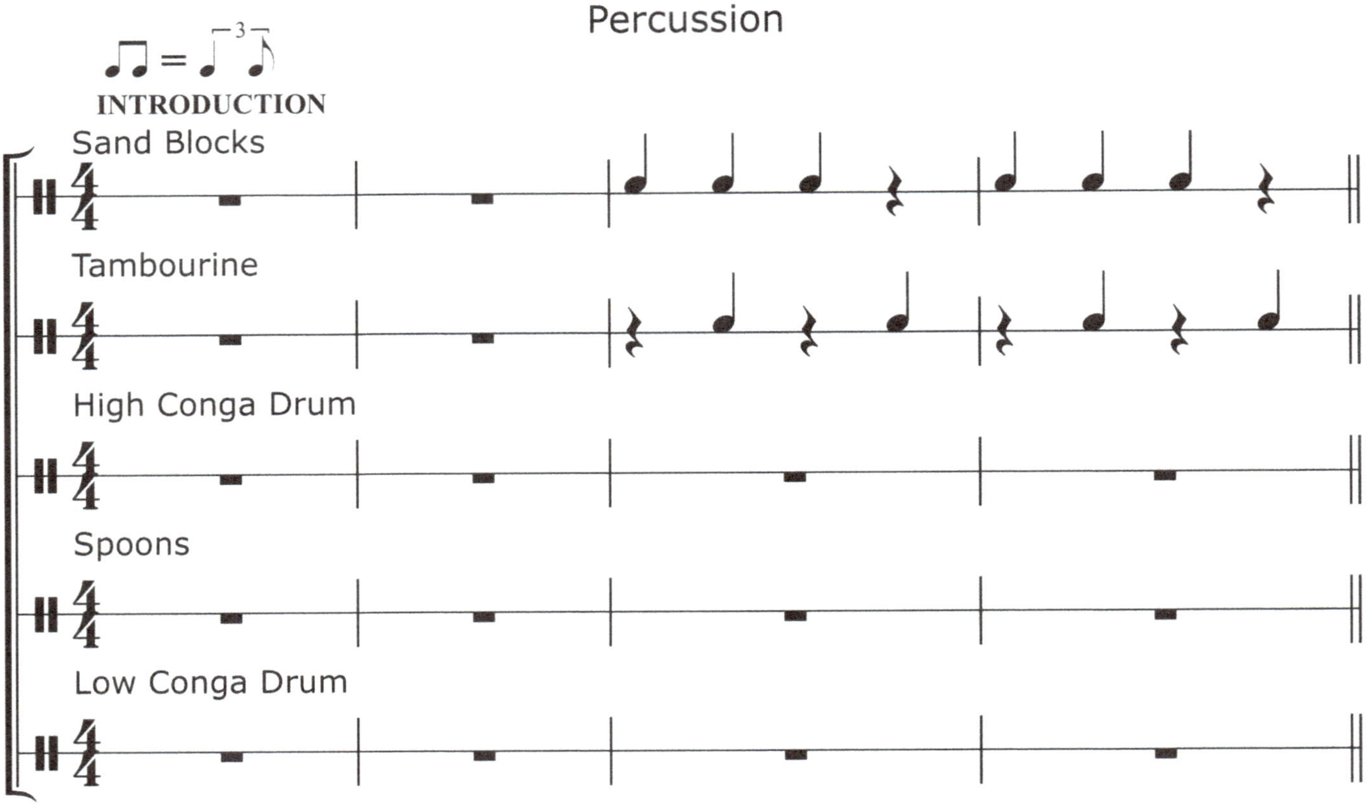

Now That's Tap

Now That's Tap

Now That's Tap

Now That's Tap

O lê lê O Bahía
(O Le O La)

Folk Song from Brazil

do
D   Solo
Da   Ba - hí - a   me   man - da - ram
1. Sent   to   me   from   Ba - hí - a,____
2. Then   I   told   him   that   I   will,____
G   Chorus
O   lê   lê   O   Ba - hí -
G   Solo
Um ces - ti - nho de ca - já,
Bas - ket full of good ca - já,
When the riv - ers run up - hill,
D   Chorus
O   lê   lê   O   Ba - hí - a,
Solo
E man - da - ram per - gun -
With a note, et ce - te -
Or when fish be - gin to
A7   Chorus
tar
ra,
fly,
O   lê   lê   O   Ba - hí - a,
Solo
Se eu que - ri - a me ca - sar.
"Will you mar - ry me?" (Ah - ha!)
Or the day be - fore I   die.
D   Chorus
O   lê   lê   O   Ba - hí -
D   Solo
a,   O   le   o   la,
A7   Chorus
O   lê   lê   O   Ba - hí - a,
Solo
O   le   o
D   Chorus
la,   O   lê   lê   O   Ba - hí - a,
1.   Solo
O   le   o
2.
a.

Peace Like a River

Phone Tag
(Hello, My Baby)

by Joe Howard and Ida Emerson
Arranged, with New Words and Music,
by Sally K. Albrecht and Jay Althouse

1st time: PART I only
2nd time: PART II only
3rd time: Sing both parts

Hel - lo, my ba - by. Hel - lo, my hon - ey.
I sit a - lone, here by the phone. I'm

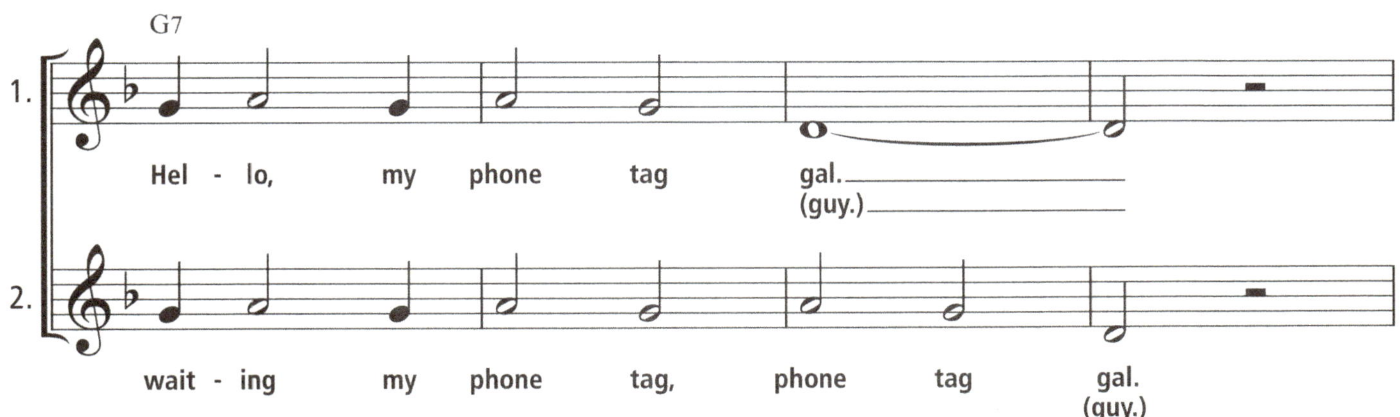

Hel - lo, my phone tag gal. (guy.)
wait - ing my phone tag, phone tag gal. (guy.)

151

Phone Tag

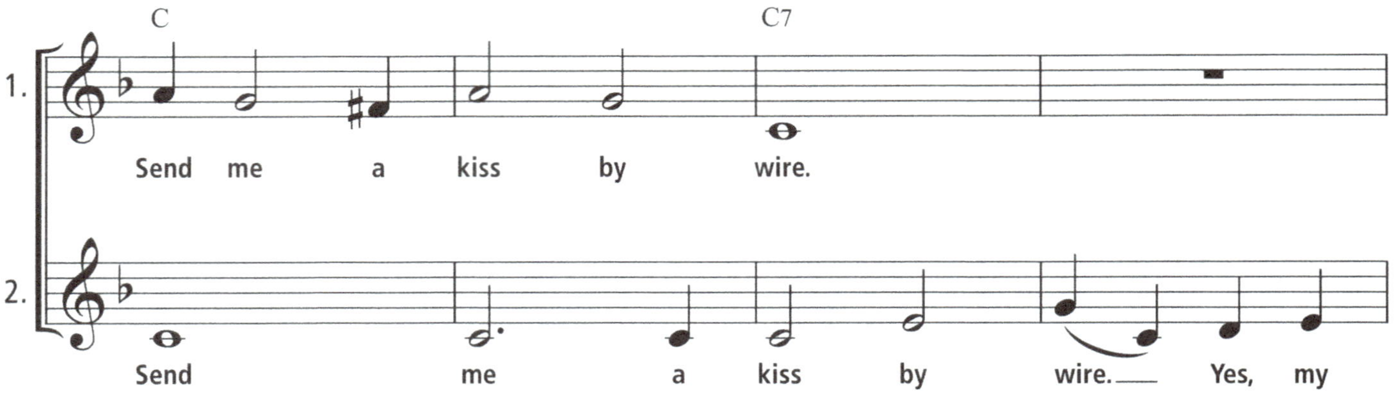
C
C7
1.
Send me a kiss by wire.
2.
Send me a kiss by wire. Yes, my

F
Fm(maj7)/A♭ Fm6/A♭
Gm7
C7
1.
Ba - by, my heart's on fire.
2.
heart is on fire. Oh, please dar - ling don't re -

F
B♭/F
F
B♭/F
F
1.
If you re - fuse me, hon - ey, you'll lose me.
2.
fuse me, or you will lose me.

Phone Tag

G7
1. Then you'll be left a - lone. Oh, ba - by,
2. Then you'll be left a - lone. Oh, ba - by,

C
C6   C7
1. tel - e - phone, and tell me I'm your
2. call me up, call me on the tel - e -

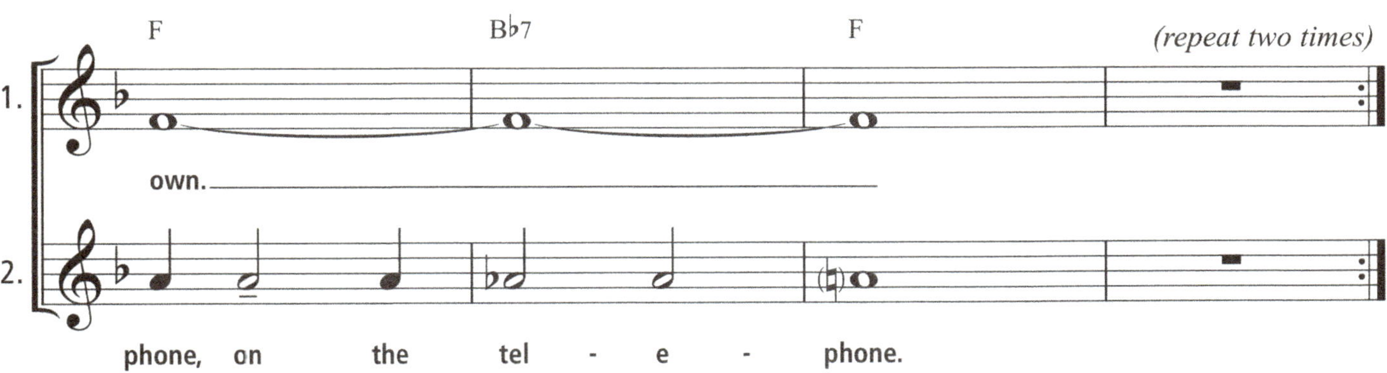

F   B♭7   F   (repeat two times)
1. own.
2. phone, on the tel - e - phone.

Play Ball!
(A Partner Song with "Take Me Out to the Ball Game")

Words by Jack Norworth
Music by Albert von Tilzer
Arranged, with new Words and Music, by
Mary Donnelly and George L. O. Strid

With excitement ♩ = c. 108
C/G
Db/Ab
Moderate waltz, in one ♩. = c. 60
1.
2. do
Charge!
Charge!
Part 2 (opt. unison)
Oh, what a day to go to the ball - park. I wan - na shout hoo -
* Hoo - ray!
ray! I like to hear the crack of the bat
as it sends the ball fly - ing back, back, back. One of these days, I'll
Hall of Fame.
play in the ma - jors. I'll make the Hall of Hall of Fame.
Till that day I'm hap - py to stay right here at the base - ball
*Optional echo group

Play Ball!

Take me out to the ball game, take me out with the
crowd. Buy me some pea - nuts and Crack - er Jack.
I don't care if I nev - er get back. Let me root, root,
root for the home team. If they don't win it's a
shame. For it's one, two, three strikes, you're
out at the old ball game!

Play Ball!

mf
C   C/G   G7sus/D   G7   C
1. Take me out to the ball game, take me out with the
mf
2. Oh, what a day to go to the ball - park. I wan - na shout hoo -

G7sus/D   G7   A   A7/E   Dm   Dm/A
1. crowd. _____ Buy me some pea - nuts and Crack - er Jack.
* Hoo - ray!
2. ray! _____ I like to hear the crack of the bat

D7   D7/F#   G   C   C/G
1. I don't care if I nev - er get back. Let me root, root, root for the
2. as it sends the ball fly - ing back, back, back. One of these days, I'll

G7sus/D   G7   C   C7/Bb   F   A7/E Dm
1. home team. If they don't win, it's a shame. For it's
Hall of Fame. _____
2. play in the ma - jors. I'll make the Hall of Hall of Fame.

156

Play Ball!

one,
two,
three strikes, you're out at the old
Till that day I'm hap - py to stay right here at the
ball game! Take me out to the old
base - ball game! Take me out to the old
ball game!
Play ball!
ball game!
Play ball!

Razzamatazz

Words and Music by Andy Beck and Brian Fisher

do—
Razz - a - ma - tazz,___ razz - a - ma - ting,___
when it's time to dance and sing,___ razz - a - ma - tazz,___
razz - a - ma - ting___ we say.
do—
Razz - a - ma - tazz,___ razz - a - ma - tance,___ ev - 'ry - bod - y

Copyright © 2007 by Alfred Music Publishing Co., Inc.
All Rights Reserved.   Printed in USA.

Razzamatazz

sing and dance, razz - a - ma - tazz, razz - a - ma - tance, to -
day. We're gon - na wig - gle, We're gon - na wig - gle,
we're gon - na wag. We'll make you we're gon - na wag. We'll make you
gig - gle when we do the rag.
gig - gle when we

Razzamatazz
A#dim6
G/B
f
C
E7/B
Razz - a - ma - tazz, __ razz - a - ma - toh, __
do the rag. __ Razz - a - ma - tazz, __ razz - a - ma - toh, __
Am
D7
Am7/G
read - y, set, 'cause here we go, __ razz - a - ma - tazz - a - ma,
read - y, set, 'cause here we go, __ razz - a - ma - tazz - a - ma,
G7
C
razz - a - ma - tazz - a - ma show!
razz - a - ma - tazz - a - ma show!
C
E7/B
A7
Wee! Wee! Wee!
Wee! Wee! Wee!

Razzamatazz

Wee!
Wah, wah, wah, wah,
Wee!
Wah, wah, wah, wah,
wop.
Ba - dop!
Wee!
wop.
Ba - dop!
Wee!
Wee!
Wee!
Wee!
Wee!
Wee!
Wee!
Wah, wah, wah, wah, wop!
Wah, wah, wah, wah, wop!

Razzamatazz

C
mf
C7
1.
We're gon - na wig - gle, ___ we're gon - na
2.
mf
We're gon - na wig - gle, ___ we're gon - na

Dm7/F
Em6   Dm7/F   D♭7
1.
wag. ___ We'll make you gig - gle ___
2.
wag. ___ We'll make you gig - gle ___

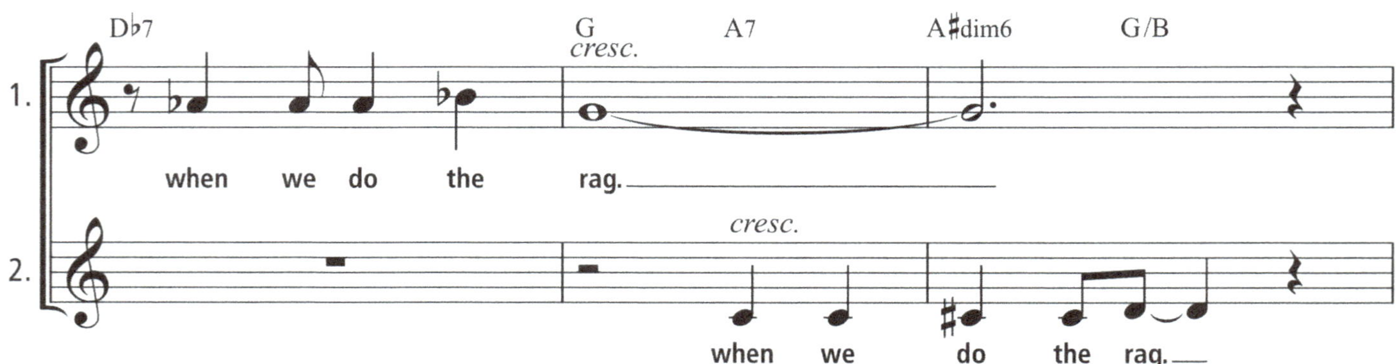

D♭7
G   A7   A♯dim6   G/B
cresc.
1.
when we do the rag. ___
cresc.
2.
when we do the rag. ___

C
E7/B   Am
f
1.
Razz - a - ma - tazz. ___ razz - a - ma - toh, ___ shake and shim - my
f
2.
Razz - a - ma - tazz. ___ razz - a - ma - toh, ___ shake and shim - my

Razzamatazz

D7
Am7/G
G7
1.
to and fro, ___ razz - a - ma-tazz - a - ma, razz - a - ma-tazz - a - ma
2.
to and fro, ___ razz - a - ma-tazz - a - ma, razz - a - ma-tazz - a - ma

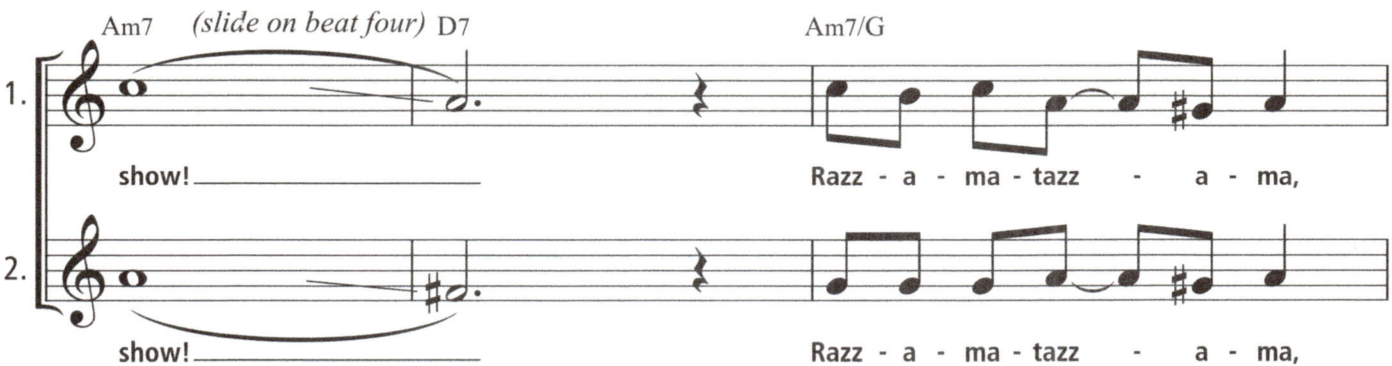

Am7
(slide on beat four) D7
Am7/G
1.
show! ___________ Razz - a - ma - tazz - a - ma,
2.
show! ___________ Razz - a - ma - tazz - a - ma,

G7
C
ff
1.
razz - a - ma - tazz - a - ma show! Razz - a - ma - tazz! __
2.
razz - a - ma - tazz - a - ma show! Razz - a - ma - tazz! __

Red River Valley

Cowboy Song from the United States

REFRAIN
Come and sit by my side if you love me,___ Do not
has - ten to bid me a - dieu; But re - mem - ber the Red Riv - er
Val - ley___ And the girl that has loved you so true.
rit. (first time only)
Fine
VERSE
1. From this val - ley they say you are go - ing,___ We will
2. Won't you think of the val - ley you're leav - ing?___ Oh, how
miss your bright eyes and sweet smile; For they say you are tak - ing the
lone - ly, how sad it will be. Oh,___ think of the fond heart you're
sun - shine,___ That bright - ens our path - way a - while.
break - ing,___ And the grief you are causing me to see.
D.C. al Fine

The Rhythm Is Gonna Get You

Words and Music by Gloria Estefan
and Enrique Garcia

VERSE
Gm
At night,— when you turn off all the lights,
No way— you can fight it ev-'ry day,
Eb
— There's no place that you can hide;— No, no,
— But no mat-ter what you say,— You know
F
— it, the rhy-thm is gon-na get— you.
Gm
At night— throw the cov-ers on your head,
No clue— of what's hap-pen-ing to you.
You pre-tend like you were dead,—
But be-fore this night is through,
The rhy-thm is gon-na get— you.

The Rhythm Is Gonna Get You

REFRAIN
Gm
Gm
Eb
Eb
F
1.
Gm
The rhy - thm is gon - na get you,— the rhy - thm is gon - na get you,— the rhy - thm is gon - na get you,—
The rhy - thm is gon - na get you— to - night!
Gm
F
2., 3.
Gm
Fine
to - night!
N.C. (vocal only)
O - eh, O - eh.—— (O - eh, O - eh.)—— O - eh, O -
D.S. al Fine
- ah. (O - eh, O - ah.) O - eh, O - eh.

Ribbons in the Sky

Words and Music by
Andy Beck

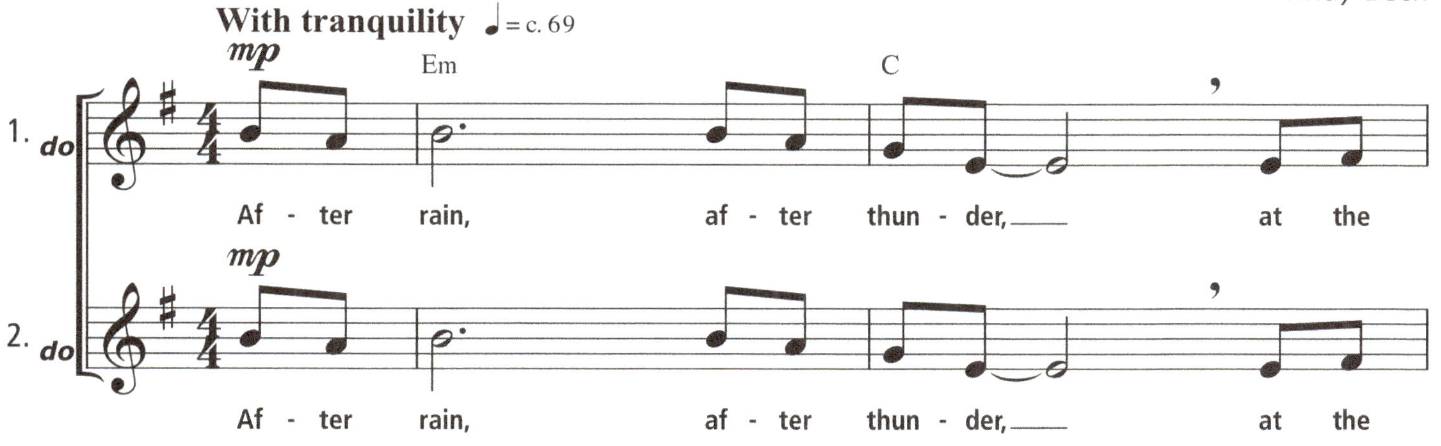

With tranquility ♩ = c. 69
mp
Em
C
1. do
Af - ter rain, af - ter thun - der, at the
mp
2. do
Af - ter rain, af - ter thun - der, at the

Am
Bm7
Em
1. calm - ing of the storm, when the sun re - turns, shin - ing
2. calm - ing of the storm, when the sun re - turns, shin - ing

C
Am
Bm7
Em
B7sus
B7
1. bright - ly, col - ored rib - bons start to form.
2. bright - ly, col - ored rib - bons start to form.

Ribbons in the Sky

mf
G   C   G   Am   D
1. Af - ter the rain   is   done,   look   for a rain - bow   in   the   sun.
mf
2. Af - ter the rain   is   done,   look   for the rain - bow   in   the   sun.

G   Am7   B   Em   decresc.
1. Af - ter the storm   com - plete - ly   pass - es   by,
decresc.
2. Af - ter the storm   com - plete - ly   pas - es   by,

C   Bm7   mp   Em   2
1. look   for a rain - bow,   rib-bons in the   sky.
mp   2
2. look   for a rain - bow,   rib-bons in the   sky.

Red   Orange
Em   C
1. Look for   red,   look for   or - ange,   look for
2. Look for   red,   look for   or - ange,

Ribbons in the Sky

Yellow
Green
Blue
Indigo
Am
Bm7
Em
1.
yel - low,   green, and   blue.   Look for in - di - go,____
2.
____ yel - low, green, and blue.   Look for in - di - go,   look for
Violet
C
Am
Bm7
1.
____ look   for vio - let,____   col - or ev - 'ry
2.
vio - let,____   ev - 'ry   col - or,   ev - 'ry
Em
B7sus
B7
mf
G
C
1.
hue.   Af - ter the rain   is   done,
mf
2.
hue.   Af - ter the rain   is   done,
G
Am
D
G
Am7
B
1.
look for a rain - bow in   the sun.   Af - ter the storm com - plete - ly   pass - es
2.
look for a rain - bow in   the sun.   Af - ter the storm com - plete - ly   pass - es

Ribbons in the Sky

Em   C   Bm7   mp
decresc.
1. by, ____________ look for a rain - bow, rib-bons in the
decresc.
2. by, ____________ look for a rain - bow,

Red   Orange   Yellow   Green
Em   decresc.   C rit.
1. sky, rib-bons in the sky.
mp   decresc.
2. rib-bons in the sky, rib-bons in the sky.

Blue   Indigo   Violet   Rainstick
Am7   Bm7   p Em
1. Look for a rain - bow, rib-bons in the sky. ____________
p
2. Look for a rain - bow, rib-bons in the sky. ____________

Riendo el río corre
(Run, Run, River)

Words and Music by Tish Hinojosa
English Words by Sue Ellen LaBelle

REFRAIN
Dm
do
Co - rre, co - rre,____ co - rre el rí - o,____ Ri -
Run, run, riv - er,____ Run, run, riv - er,____ With
Gm   Dm
en - do el rí - o____ co - rre.____
laugh - ter runs____ the____ riv - er.____
Last time To Coda
Co - rre, co - rre,____ co - rre el rí - o,____ Ri -
Run, run, riv - er,____ Run, run, riv - er,____ With
Gm   Dm
en - do el rí - o____ co - rre.____
laugh - ter runs____ the____ riv - er.

Riendo el río corre

VERSE
Gm7
Gm7
1. Cuén - ta - me de las mon - ta - ñas
2. Sa - bes tú de la dis - tan - cia que
1. Tell a - bout the high moun - tains
2. Tell a - bout the great dis - tance you've

Dm
de tu em - pe zar,
pien - sas al - can - zar,
where your jour - ney be - gan,
gone to reach the sea,

Gm7
Cuén - ta - me de pie - dra y pe - na
Co - mo sue - ño de la lu - na que
Tell a - bout the pla - ces you
Whis - p'rings of your tra - vels seem

Dm
A
D.C. al Coda
que lle - vas al mar.
me das para so - ñar.
passed a - long the way.
like a dream to me.

Coda
Gm
A7
Dm
en - do el rí - o co - rre.
laugh - ter runs the riv - er.

Rockin' Pneumonia and the Boogie Woogie Flu

Words and Music by
Huey P. Smith

Rock ♩ = 120
mf
Ab7
Eb7sus
1. do
I wan - na jump but I'm a - fraid I'll fall,
mf
2. do
I wan - na jump but I'm a - fraid I'll fall,

Ab7
Eb7sus
Ab7
Eb7sus
1.
I wan - na hol - ler but the joint's too small.
2.
I wan - na hol - ler but the joint's too small.

Ab7
Eb7
Bbm7sus
1.
Jump and rhy - thm's got a
2.
Jump and rhy - thm's got a

Rockin' Pneumonia
and the Boogie Woogie Flu

Eb7
f Gb7 G7 Ab7
1. hold on me too,— I've got the rock - in' pneu - mo - nia and the
f
2. hold of me too,— I've got the rock - in' pneu - mo - nia and the

N.C.
Ab7
Eb7sus
1. boo - gie woo - gie flu.
2. boo - gie woo - gie flu. Want some lov - in', ba - by, that ain't all,—

Ab7 Eb7sus Ab7 Eb7sus
2. — I wan - na kiss her but she's way— too tall.—

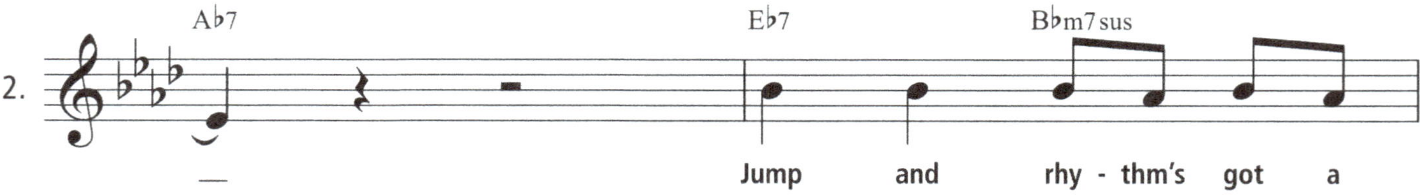

Ab7 Eb7 Bbm7sus
2. — Jump and rhy - thm's got a

Eb7(#9) Eb7 f Gb7 G7 Ab7
2. hold on me too,— I've got the rock - in' pneu - mo - nia and the

Rockin' Pneumonia
and the Boogie Woogie Flu

I wan - na squeeze him but he's way too low, __
boo - gie woo - gie flu.

__ I would be run - nin' but my feet's_ too slow. __

Jump and rhy - thm's got a hold on me too, __ I've got the
Jump and rhy - thm's got a hold on me too, __ I've got the

rock - in' pneu - mo - nia and the boo - gie woo - gie flu. Got the rock -
rock - in' pneu - mo - nia and the boo - gie woo - gie flu.

Rockin' Pneumonia
and the Boogie Woogie Flu

Ab13   Eb13   Ab13   Eb+9   Ab13
- in' pneu - mo - nia,   and the boo -
Got the rock - in' pneu - mo - nia,

Ab13   Eb13   Ab13   Db13
gie woo - gie flu.   Got the rock -
mf
and the boo - gie woo - gie flu.

Db13   Ab+7(#9)   Db13   Ab13
- in' pneu - mo - nia,   and the boo -
Got the rock - in' pneu - mo - nia,

Ab13   Eb13   Ab13
gie woo - gie flu.
and the boo - gie woo - gie flu.

Rockin' Pneumonia
and the Boogie Woogie Flu

Eb13   Bbm9   Eb9   Gb13 G13 Ab13
1. Jump   and   rhy-thm's go a   hold   on   me   too,___   I've   got   the
2. Jump   and   rhy-thm's got a   hold   on   me   too,___   I've   got   the

Ab13   f Bb13
1. rock-in' pneu-mo - nia and the boo-gie woo-gie flu. Ba-by,
2. rock-in' pneu-mo - nia and the boo-gie woo-gie flu. Ba-by,

Bb13   F+7(#9)   Bb13   F+7(#9)
1. com-in' now I'm hur-ry-in' home,___ I know she'll
2. com-in' now I'm hur-ry-in' home,___ I know she'll

Bb13   F+7(#9)   Bb13   N.C.
1. leave me 'cuz I'm tak-in' too long.___
2. leave me 'cuz I'm tak-in' too long.___

Rockin' Pneumonia and the Boogie Woogie Flu

Jump and rhy-thm's got a hold on me too. _ Jump and rhy-thm's got a
Jump and rhy-thm's got a

hold on me too, _ Jump and rhy - thm's got a
hold on me too, _ Jump and rhy - thm's got a

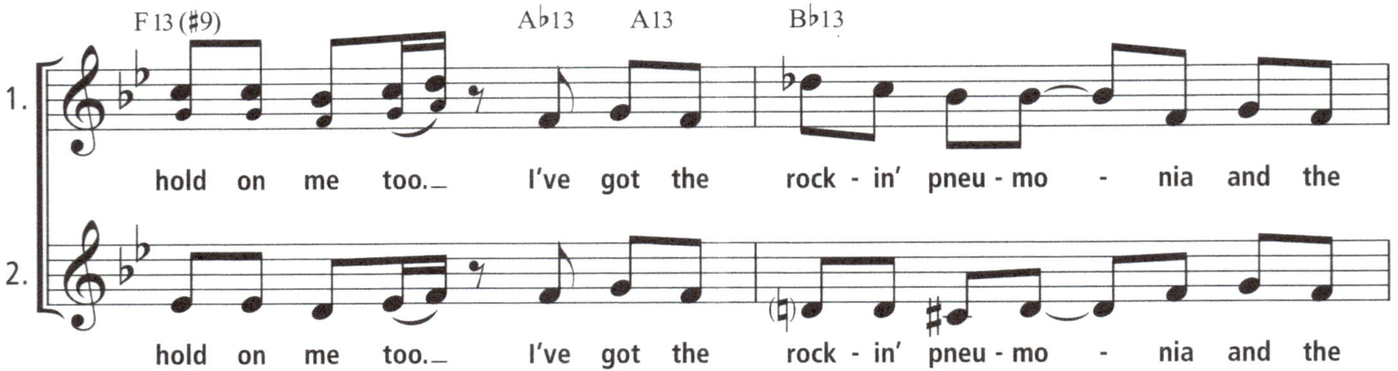
hold on me too. _ I've got the rock - in' pneu - mo - nia and the
hold on me too. _ I've got the rock - in' pneu - mo - nia and the

boo - gie _______ woo - gie flu.
boo - gie _______ woo - gie flu.

178

Santa Mash-Up
Santa Is the Man • Santa Fever

Music by Lois Brownsey
and Marti Lunn Lantz
Driving disco ♩ = c. 132
Fm
Eb/F
Fm
Eb/F
Woo hoo! Woo hoo!
Woo hoo! Woo hoo!
Fm
Eb/F
Fm
Eb/F
San - ta fe - ver, I've got the fe - ver now. San - ta fe - ver, uh
San - ta fe - ver, I've got the fe - ver now. San - ta fe - ver, uh
Fm
Eb
F
Fm
Eb
Fm
huh, uh huh. San - ta fe - ver, I'm a be - liev - er now,
huh, uh huh. San - ta fe - ver, I'm a be - liev - er now,
Fm
Eb
Fm
Cm7
Fm
San - ta fe - ver is com - in' to town. Woo hoo!
San - ta fe - ver. (stomp stomp clap)

Santa Mash-Up

(stomp stomp clap)
(stomp stomp clap)
(stomp stomp clap)
Woo hoo!
Santa is the man, and he's got a plan, I'm his big - gest
Santa is the man, and he's got a plan, I'm his big - gest
fan, and he's com - in' at Christ - mas.
fan, and he's com - in' at Christ - mas.
Woo hoo!
(stomp stomp clap)
(stomp stomp clap)
(stomp stomp clap)
Woo hoo!

Santa Mash-Up

(stomp stomp clap) The big man's com-in', so you got-ta be good. He's
He rocks all the kids in the cool, he's hot, he's in the groove.
neigh-bor - hood. We've got to dance, just got to move.
sub. mp Catch the fe - ver! Catch the
sub. mp cresc. Catch the fe - ver! Catch the

Santa Mash-Up

fe - ver! Santa is the man. (stomp stomp clap)
fe - ver! (stomp stomp clap) I've got the fe - ver now,
Santa is the man. (stomp stomp clap) Santa is the man.
(stomp stomp clap) uh huh, uh huh. (stomp stomp clap)
(stomp stomp clap) Santa is the man. (stomp stomp clap)
I'm a be - liev - er now, (stomp stomp clap) uh huh, uh huh.

San - ta fe - ver, I've got the fe - ver now. San - ta fe - ver, uh
San - ta is the man, and he's got a plan, I'm his big - gest fan, and he's com - in' at

Santa Mash-Up

huh, uh huh. San - ta fe - ver, I'm a be - liev - er now,
Christ - mas. San - ta is the man, and he's got a plan, I'm his big - gest
San - ta fe - ver is com - in' to town. Woo hoo!
fan and he's com - in' at Christ - mas. (stomp stomp clap)
(stomp stomp clap) (stomp stomp clap)
(stomp stomp clap) Woo hoo!
San - ta is the man, and he's com - in' to town!
San - ta is the man, and he's com - in' to town!

Scarborough Fair

Folk Song from England

Dm   C   Dm
1. Are you go - ing to Scar - bor - ough Fair?
2. Tell her to make me a cam - bric shirt;
3. Tell her to wash it in yon - der well;
F   G   Dm
Pars - ley, sage, rose - mar - y and thyme.
Re -
With -
Where
Dm   F   C
mem - ber me to one who lives there;
out a seam or fine nee - dle work;
nev - er rain or wa - ter fell;
Dm   C   Am   Dm
She once was a true love of mine.

Scattin' A-Round

Traditional Round
Arranged by Will Schmid

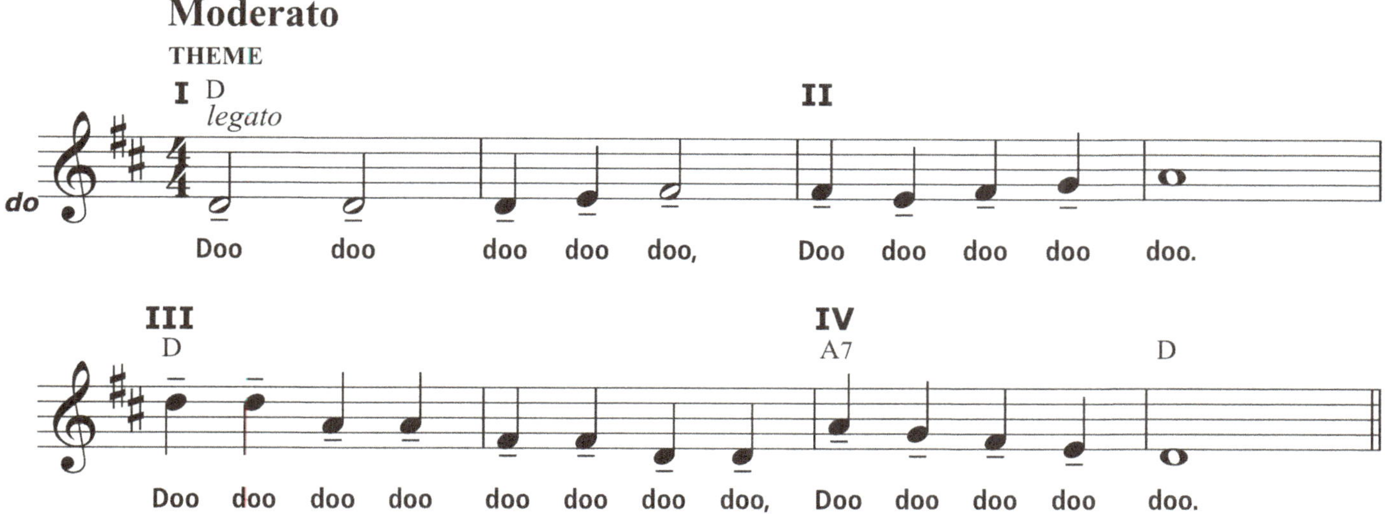

Moderato
THEME
I
II
III
IV
Doo doo doo doo doo, Doo doo doo doo doo.
Doo doo doo doo doo doo doo doo, Doo doo doo doo doo.

Allegro
VARIATION 1
I
II
Doot doot doot doo-wah, Doot doot doot doo-wah.

III
IV
Doot doot doot doot doot doo-wah, Doot doot doot-n-doo-wah.

Scattin' A-Round

Presto
VARIATION 2
I
D
swing style
II
Doo - doot   doo - doot   doo - wah,   Doo - doot   doo - wah.

III
D
IV
A7
D
doo - doot   doo - doot   doo - doo - doot,   Doo - doot   doo - wah.

(Finger snaps on beats 2 and 4)
D   X   X   X   X
Optional ostinato
for Variations 1 and 2
Doot   Doot   doot   doo doot   doot   doot

Sha Sha Sha

Music by Edward Pearsall

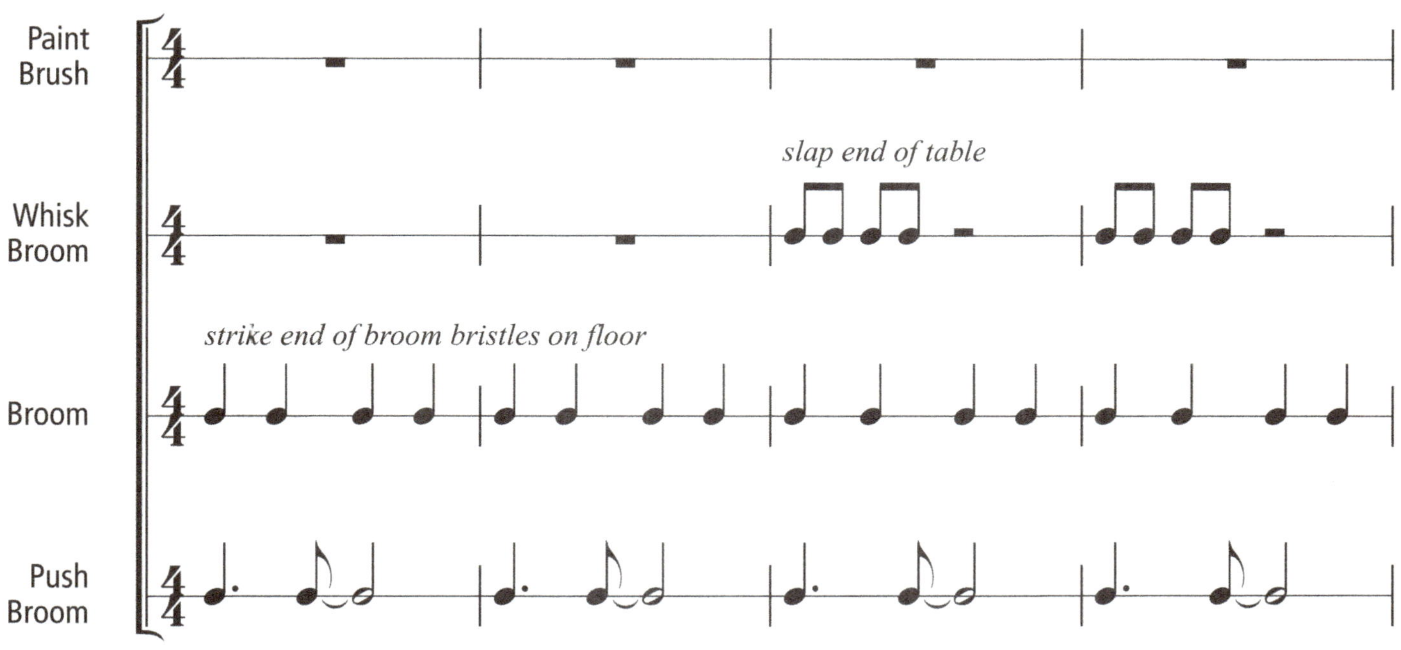

Sha Sha Sha

sweep
tap
simile

1.
2.

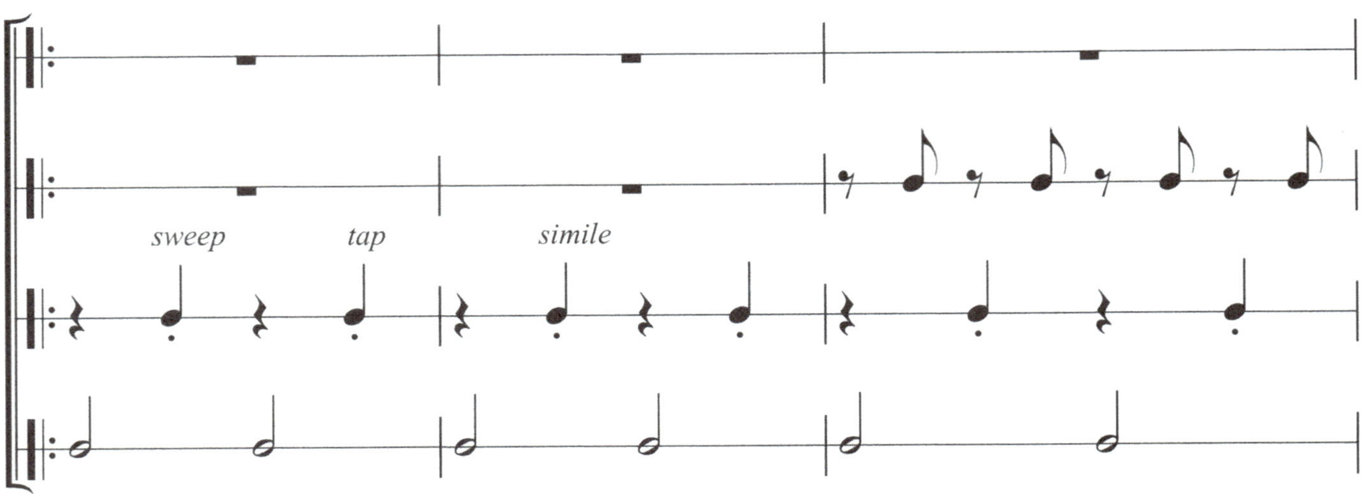

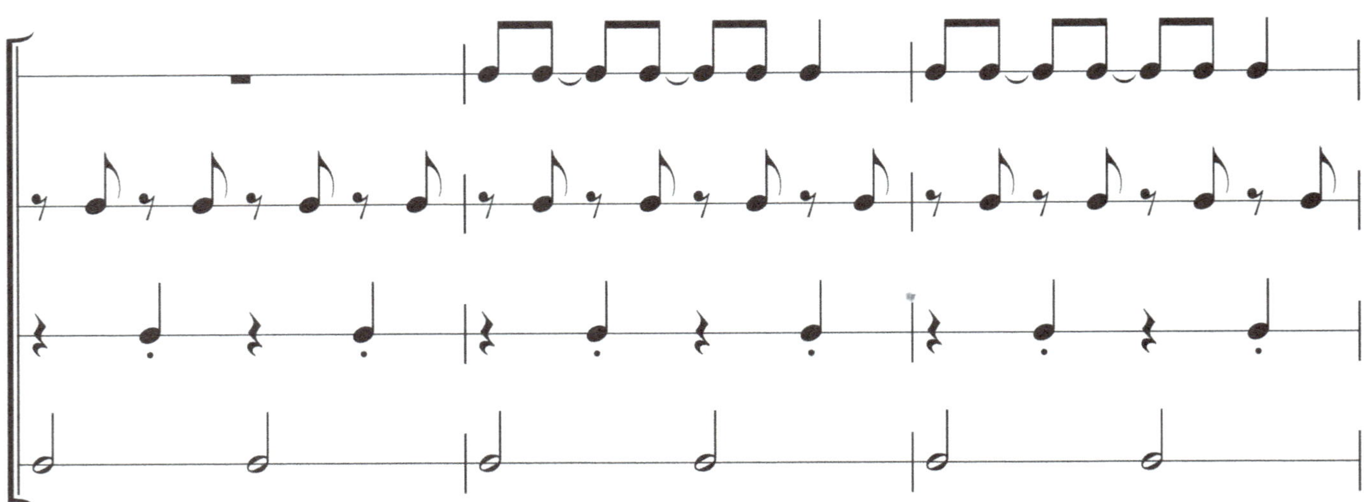

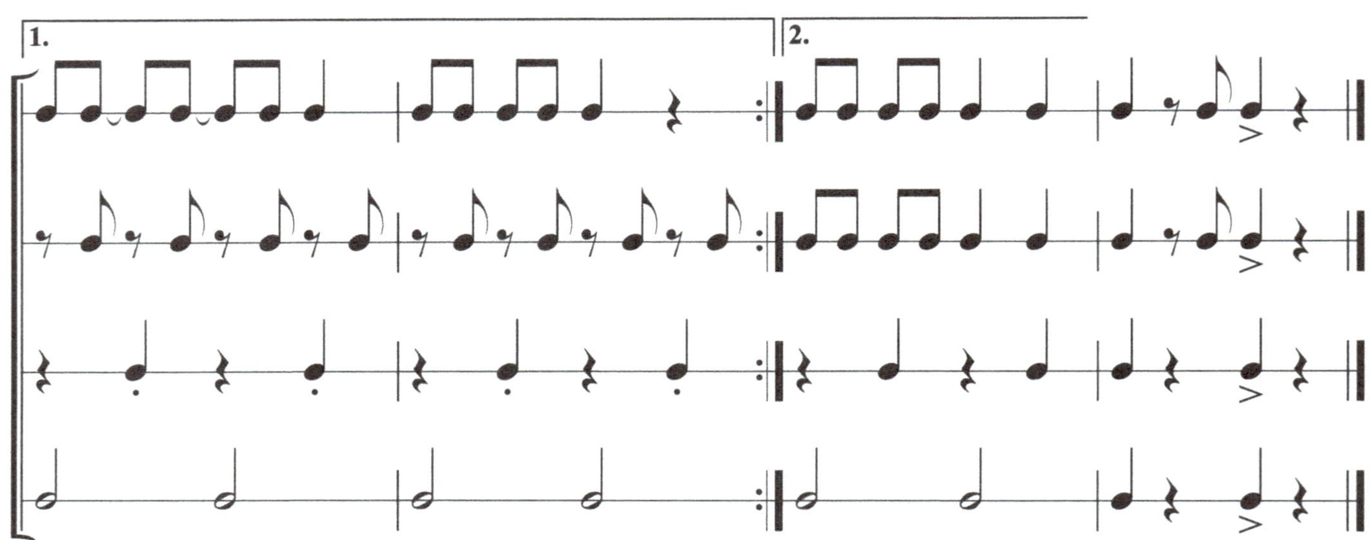

Sha Sha Sha
Recorder Ensemble

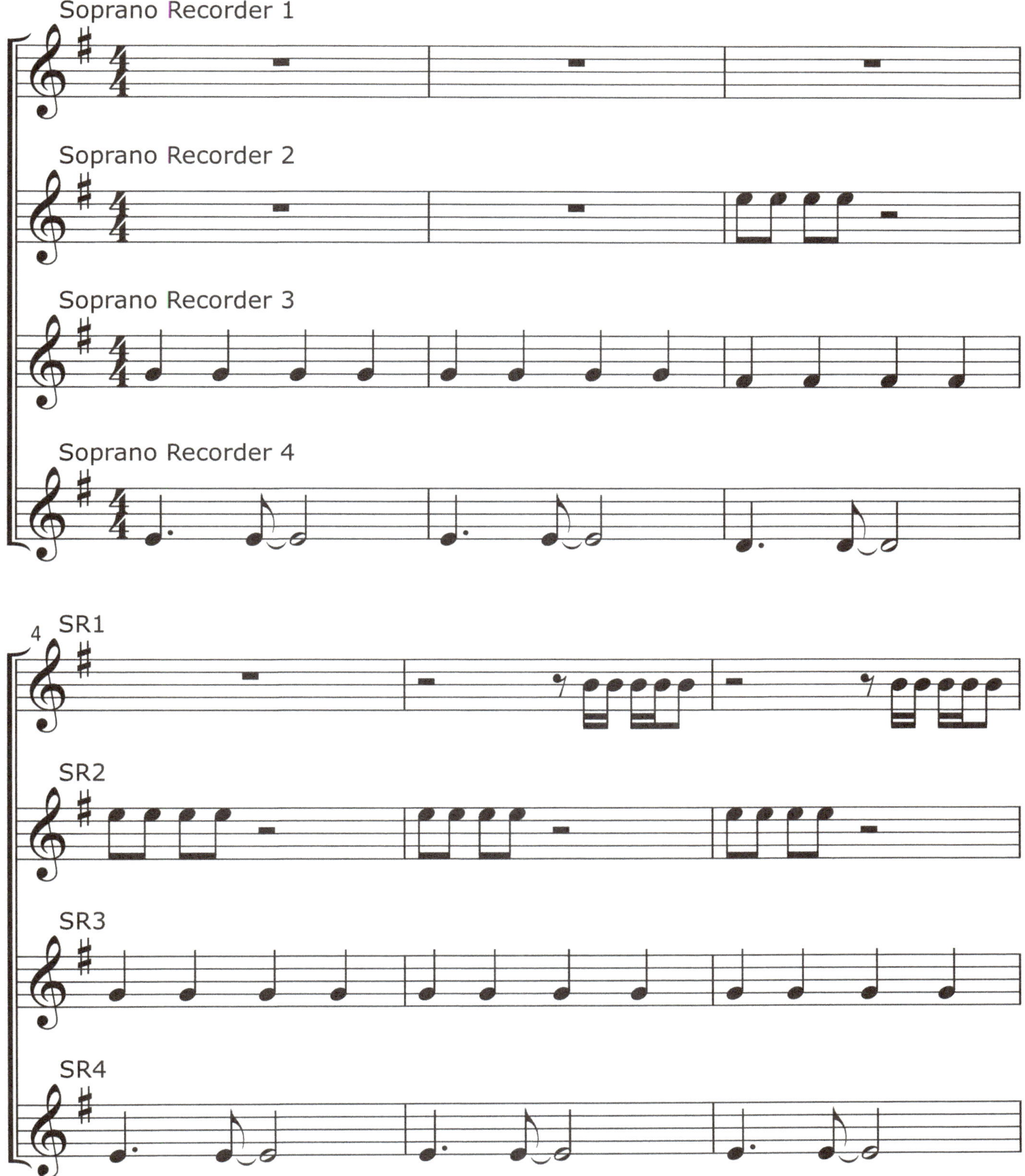

Sha Sha Sha

7
SR1
SR2
SR3
SR4

9
SR1
SR2
SR3
SR4

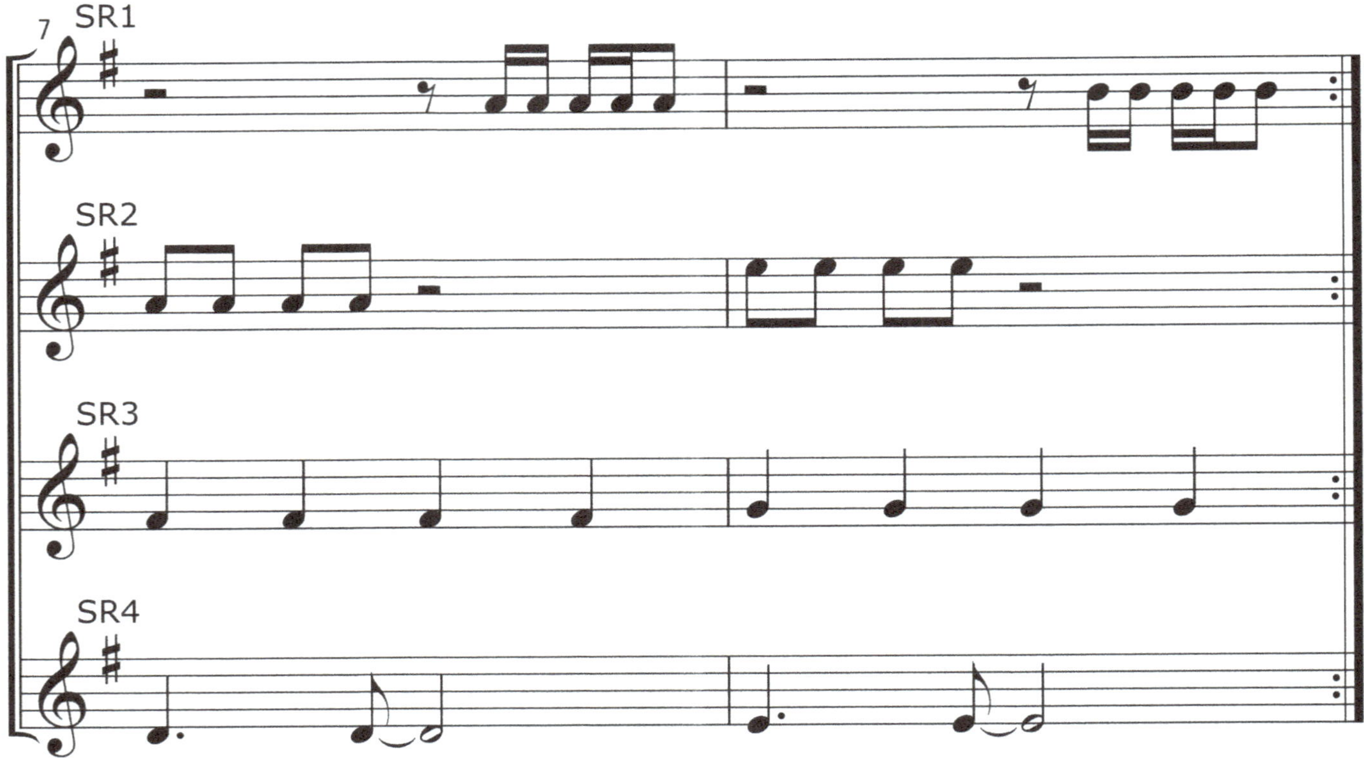

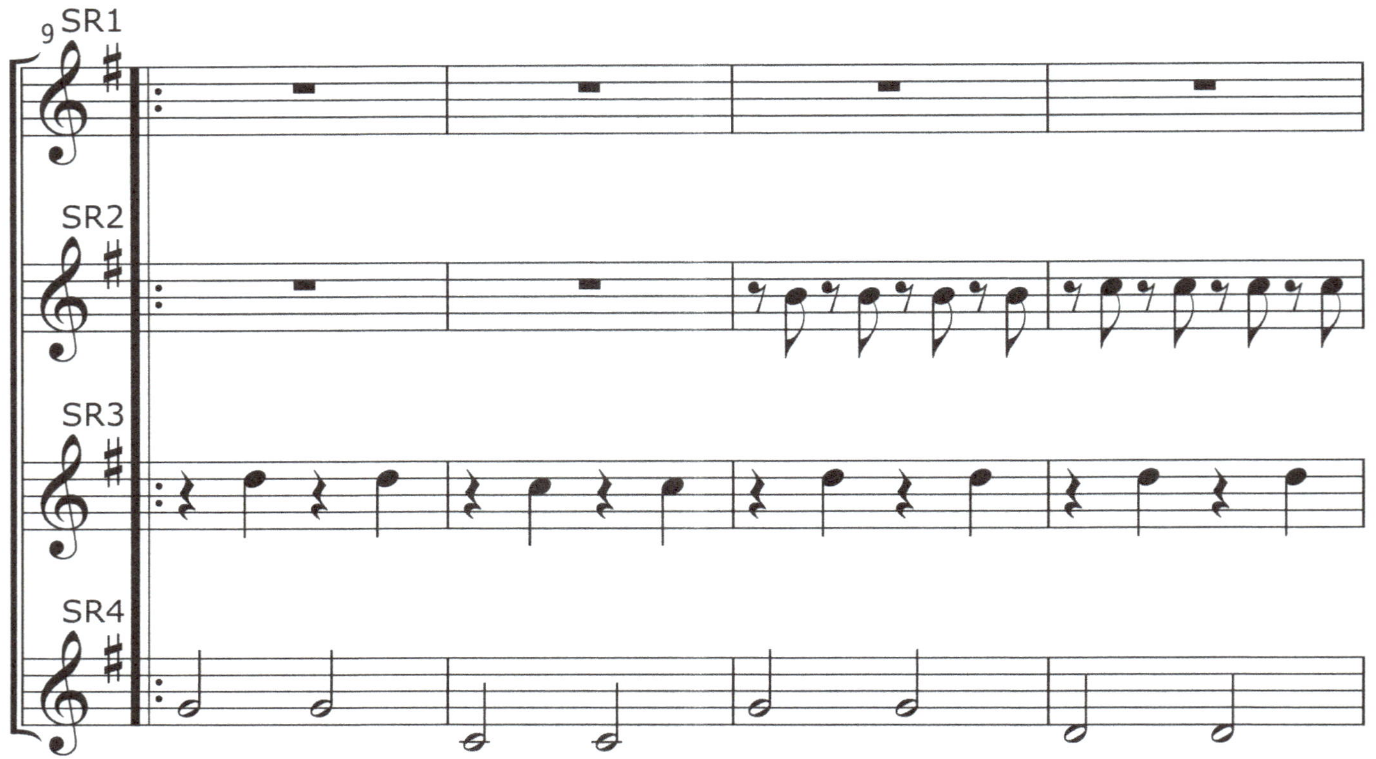

Sha Sha Sha

Sha Sha Sha
SR1
SR2
SR3
SR4
1.
2.
13
16

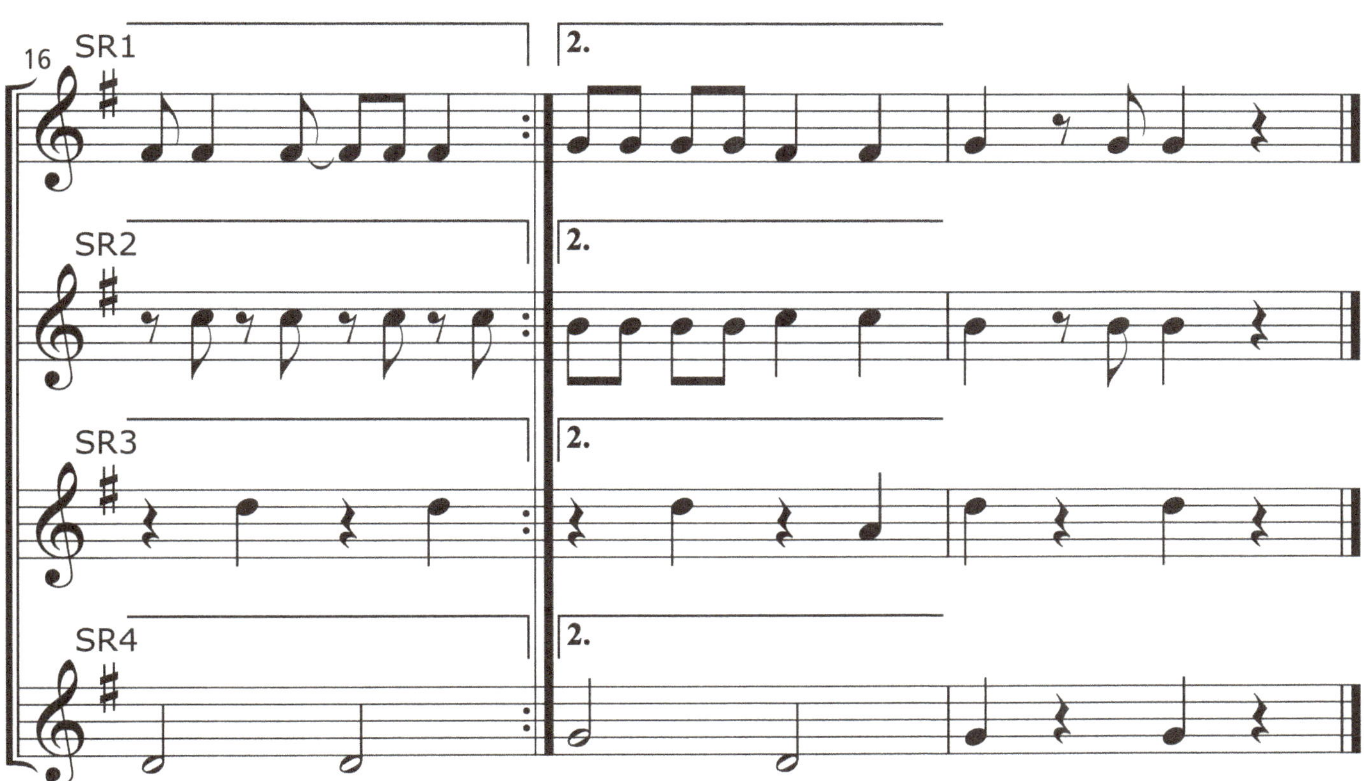

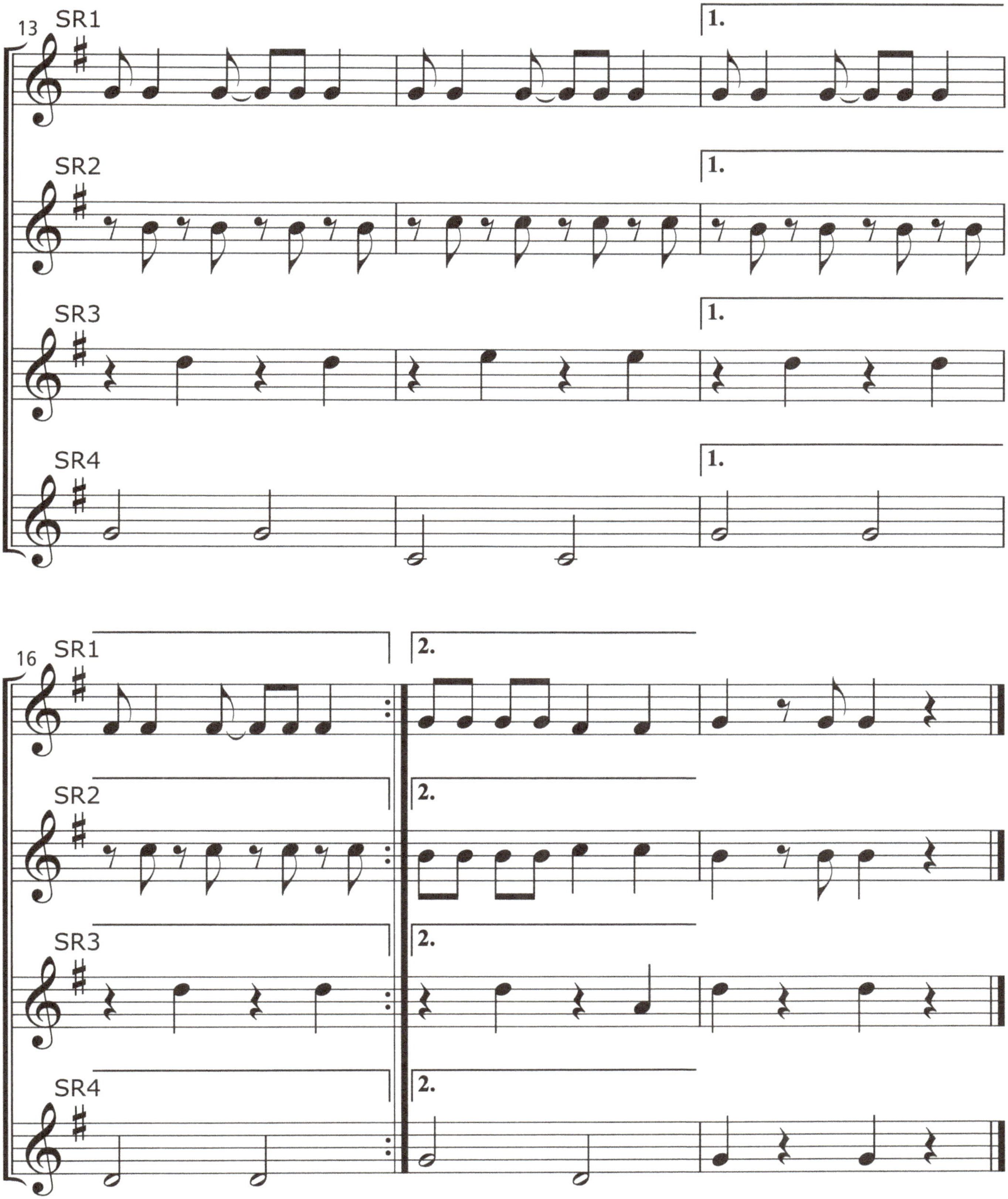

Shake, Rattle and Roll

Words and Music by Charles Calhoun
Arranged, with New Words and Music,
by Sally K. Albrecht

PART I (or unis.)
C6
Get out from that kitch-en and rat-tle those pots and pans,
C6   F9   C6
get out from that kitch-en and rat-tle those pots and pans.
C6   Dm7   F/G   C6
Well, roll my break-fast, 'cause I'm a hun-gry man.
C6
I said shake, rat-tle and roll, I said shake, rat-tle and roll,
C6   F9   C6
I said shake, rat-tle and roll, I said shake, rat-tle and roll.
C6   Dm7   G7(#9)   C6
You nev-er do noth-in' to save your dog-gone soul.

Shake, Rattle and Roll

PART II (or unis.)
Who's that cook - in' in my kitch - en? Get out! Get out!
Get out! Get out! Who's that cook - in' in my kitch - en?
Get out! Get out! Get out! Get out! Roll my break - fast, 'cause
I'm a hun - gry man. I said shake, shake,
rat - tle and roll___ I said shake, shake, rat - tle and roll___ I said
shake, shake, rat - tle and roll___ I said shake, shake,

Shake, Rattle and Roll

C6   Dm7   G7(♯9)   C6
rat-tle and roll.   You nev-er do noth-in'   to   save your dog-gone soul.

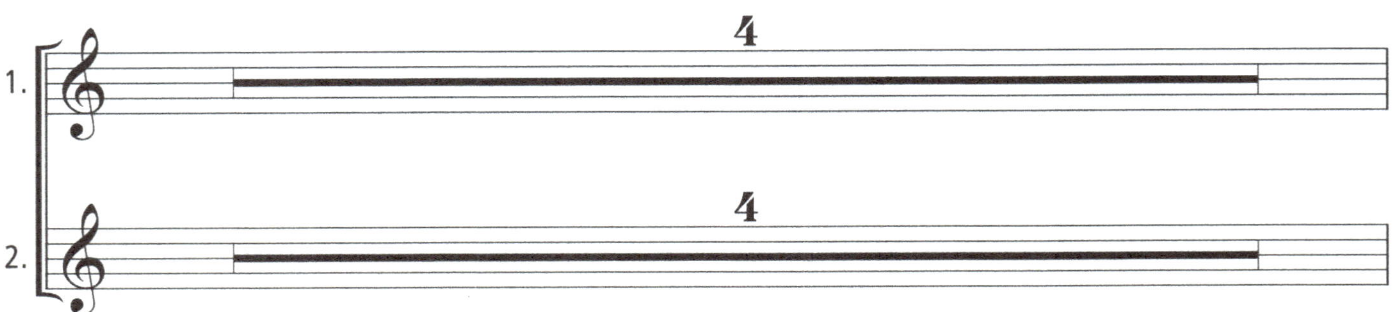

4
4

C6
f
Get out from that kitch-en and   rat-tle those   pots   and   pans,
f
Who's   that   cook - in'   in   my   kitch - en?

C6   F9
get   out from that   kitch-en and
Get out!   Get out!   Get out!   Get out!   Who's   that   cook - in'

194

Shake, Rattle and Roll

F9   C6
rat - tle those pots and pans.___   Well,
in my kitch-en?   Get out! Get out!   Get out! Get out!
Dm7   F/G   C6
roll my break-fast, 'cause I'm a hun - gry man.
Roll my break-fast, 'cause I'm a hun - gry man.
C6
I said shake, rat - tle and roll,___   I said
I said shake, shake, rat - tle and roll___ I said
C6   F9
shake, rat - tle and roll,___   I said shake, rat - tle and roll,
shake, shake, rat - tle and roll___ I said shake, shake,

Shake, Rattle and Roll

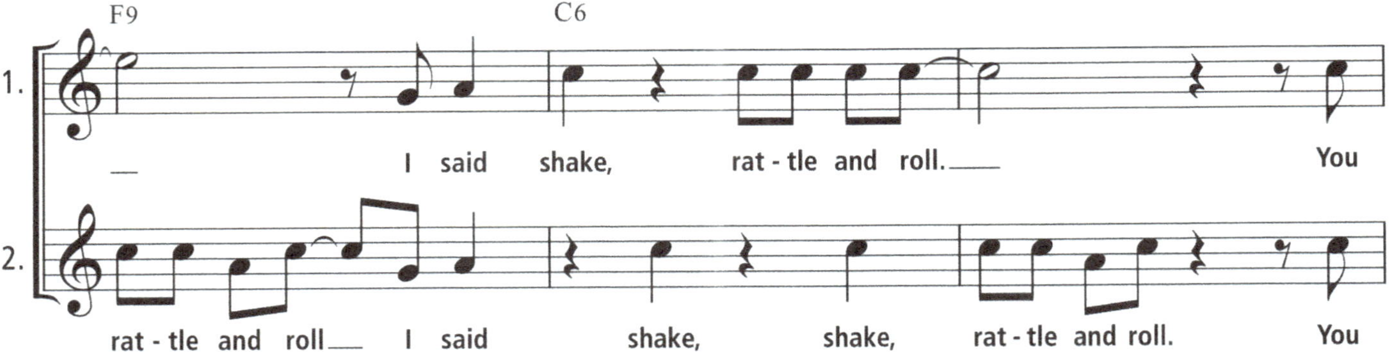

F9
C6
1.
I said shake, rat - tle and roll.___ You
2.
rat - tle and roll___ I said shake, shake, rat - tle and roll. You

Dm7
G7(♯9)
1.
nev - er do noth - in' to save your dog - gone
2.
nev - er do noth - in' to save your dog - gone

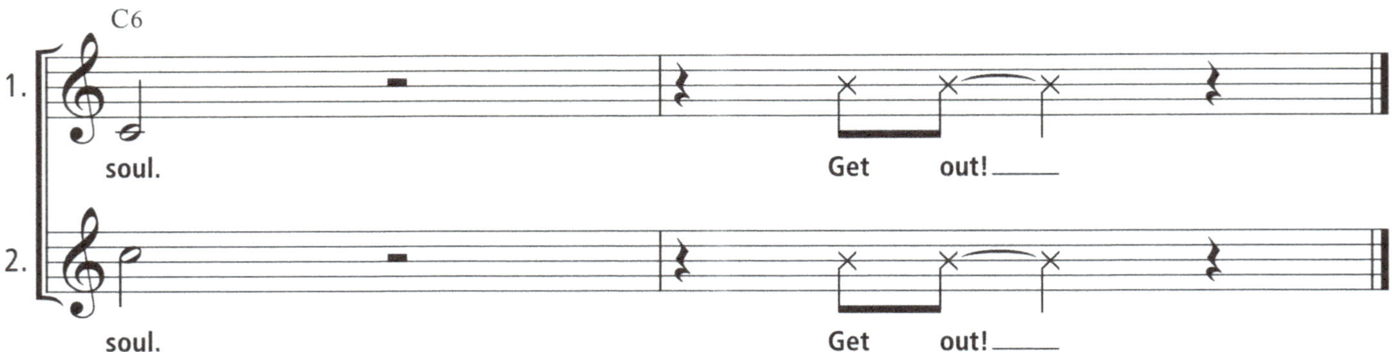

C6
1.
soul. Get out!___
2.
soul. Get out!___

Sing in Harmony!

Words and Music by
Stephen A. Paparo

Swing!
1. do Mu - sic, mu - sic makes the world go a - round.___ If you
1. lis - ten close - ly, you can hear___ the sound:___
1. Doot doot doo da dot doo wee.___
1. We can sing in har - mo - ny!___
2. I've got rhy-thm. I've got mu - sic. Won't you sing a - long with me?_
2. ___ You've got rhy - thm. You've got mu - sic.

Sing in Harmony!

And if we put our songs to -
We can sing in har - mo - ny!______ And if we put our songs to -

geth - er,______ oh, what a joy______ it would be.______
geth - er,______ oh, what a joy______ it would be.______

______ 'Cuz when we put our songs to -
______ 'Cuz when we put our songs to -

geth - er,________ we'll be sing - in' in har - mo - ny!
geth - er,________ we'll be sing - in' in har - mo - ny!______

Sing in Harmony!

F6   Gm9   C7
1. Mu - sic, mu - sic makes the world go a - round.___ If you
2. I've got rhy - thm. I've got mu - sic.

F6   Gm9   C7   F   F7/A
1. lis - ten close - ly, you can hear ___ the sound: Doot dot doo da
2. Won't you sing a - long with me?___ You've got rhy - thm.

Bb   Gm9   F/C   C7   F   C7(b13)
1. dot doo wee.___ We can sing in har - mo - ny!___
2. You've got mu - sic. We can sing in har - mo - ny!___

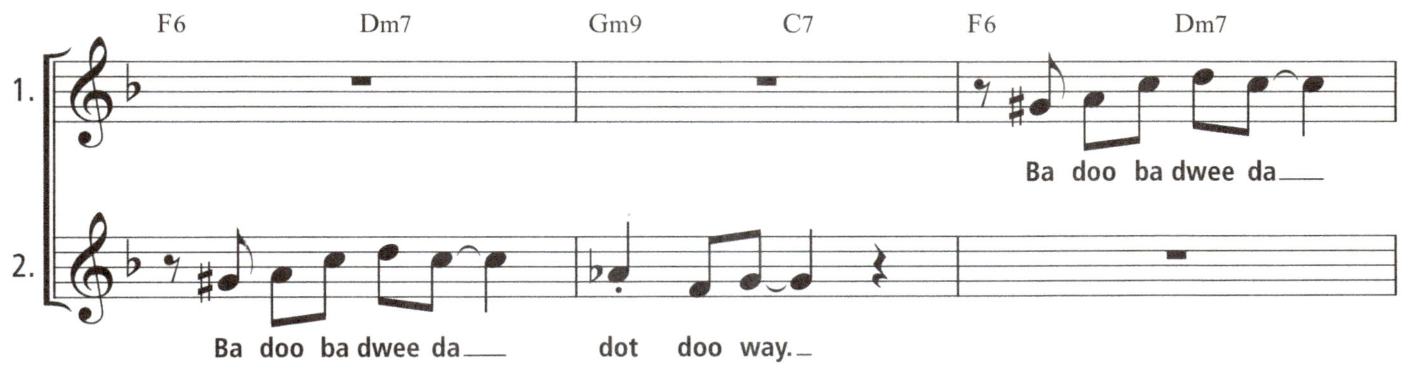

F6   Dm7   Gm9   C7   F6   Dm7
1. Ba doo ba dwee da ___
2. Ba doo ba dwee da ___ dot doo way.___

Sing in Harmony!

Gm9   C7   F cresc.   F7/A   B♭   Gm7(♭5)

1. dot doo way.__ Da ba da ba dwee ba da ba doo wah,

2. Doo wah ba da ba doo ba day,__

f F/C   F6   mf F7/C   B♭   B♭m

1. da ba dot dot doo dot. And if we put our songs to-

f
2. da ba dot dot doo dot. Doo wah

mp

Am7   Dm7   Gm9   C13

1. geth-er,_____ oh, what a joy___ it would be.___

mf
2. doo ba doo wee,___ oh, what a joy___ it would be.___

F6   F7/C   B♭   B♭m   Am7   D7   mf

mp
1. __ Doo wah doo ba doo wee,___ we'll be

2. __ 'Cuz when we put our songs to-geth-er,__________ we'll be

Sing in Harmony!

G
cresc.
C7
D7
sing - in' in har - mo - ny!
cresc.
sing - in' in har - mo - ny!

f
G6
Em7
Am9
D7
Mu - sic, mu - sic makes the world go a - round. If you
f
I've got rhy - thm. I've got mu - sic.

G6
Em7
Am9
D7
lis - ten close - ly, you can hear the sound:
Won't you sing a - long with me?

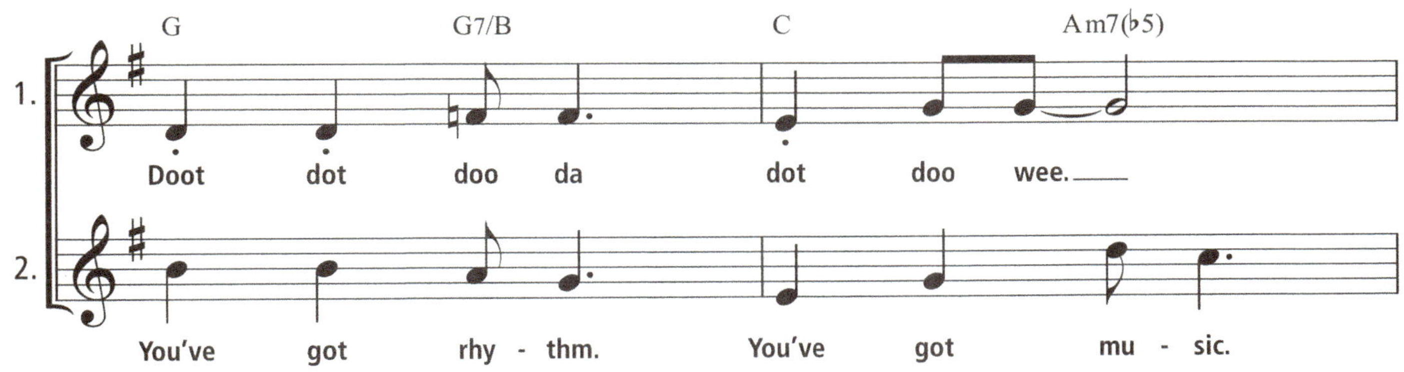

G
G7/B
C
Am7(♭5)
Doot dot doo da dot doo wee.
You've got rhy - thm. You've got mu - sic.

Sing in Harmony!

We can sing in har - mo - ny, har - mo - ny!
We can sing in har - mo - ny, har - mo - ny!

We can sing in har - mo - ny, oh yeah!
We can sing in har - mo - ny, oh yeah!

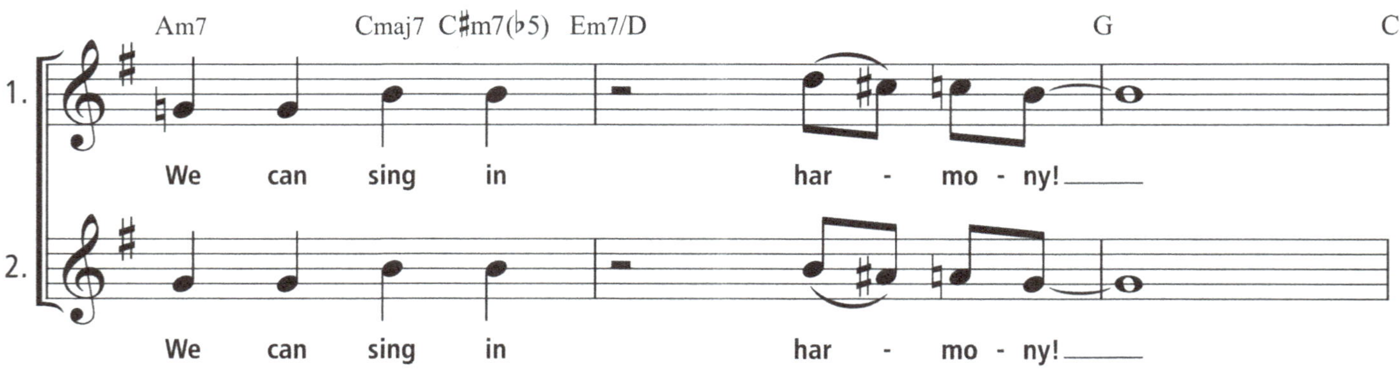

We can sing in har - mo - ny!
We can sing in har - mo - ny!

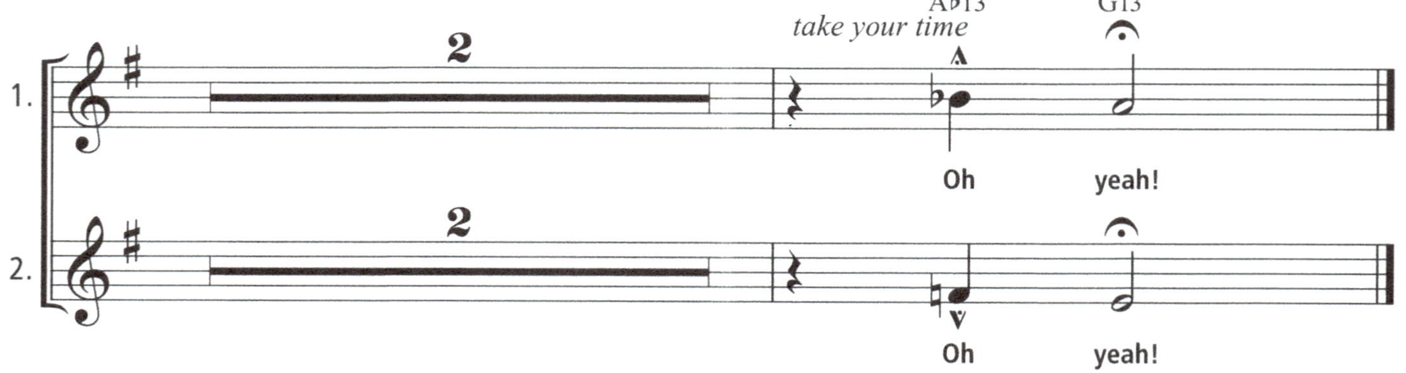

take your time
Oh yeah!
Oh yeah!

Siyahamba

Traditional Freedom Song from South Africa
Arranged by Rick Baitz

(Part 2 enters 2nd time)
G   C   G
Si - ya - hamb' - e - ku - kha - nye - ni kwen - khos'__ Si - ya -
We are walk - ing in the light__ of God.__ We are
(Part 3, last time only)
Si - ya - ham - ba   Si - ya - ham - ba
D   G
hamb'- e - ku - kha - nye - ni kwen - khos'__   Si - ya - hamb' - e - ku - kha -
walk-ing in the light__ of God.__   We are walk - ing in the
Si - ya - ham - ba   Si - ya - ham - ba   Si - ya - ham - ba
C   G   D   G
nye - ni kwen - khos'__ Si - ya - hamb'e - ku - kha - nye - ni kwen - khos'__   Si - ya -
light__ of God.__ We are walk-ing in the light__ of God.__
Si - ya - ham - ba   Si - ya - ham - ba   Si - ya - ham - ba

Siyahamba

ham-ba___   Si - ya - ham-ba___   Si - ya - hamb'e - ku-kha-nye-ni kwen-khos'
We are walk-ing in the light_ of God.
Si - ya-ham-ba   Si - ya-ham-ba   Si - ya-ham-ba

Si - ya - ham-ba___   Si - ya - ham-ba___   Si - ya -
We are
Si - ya-ham-ba   Si - ya-ham-ba   Si - ya-ham-ba

Last time to Coda
1.
2.
hamb'-e - ku-kha - nye-ni kwen-khos'___   Si - ya -   Si - ya
walk-ing in the light_ of God.___   We are
Si - ya-ham-ba

Siyahamba

G
C
D
ham-ba   Si - ya - ham-ba   Si - ya - ham-ba   Si - ya -

1.
D   G
2.
D   G
ham-ba   Si - ya - ham-ba   Si - ya - ham-ba___   Si - ya -
(Part 3, optional)
Si - ya-ham-ba___

D.S. al Coda
G   C   D
ham-ba___   Si - ya - ham-ba___   Si - ya - ham-ba___   Si - ya -
We are
Si - ya-ham-ba___   Si - ya-ham-ba___   Si - ya-ham-ba

Siyahamba

Coda
G
G
C
Si - ya - ham-ba
Si - ya - ham-ba
Si - ya -
Si - ya-ham-ba
Si - ya-ham-ba
Si - ya-ham-ba

C
D
1.–3.
G
ham - ba
Si - ya - ham - ba
Si - ya -
Si - ya - ham - ba
Si - ya - ham - ba

4.
D
G
ham - ba
Si - ya - ham - ba
Si - ya - ham - ba
Si - ya - ham - ba

Step Too My Lou

By José Antonio Diaz

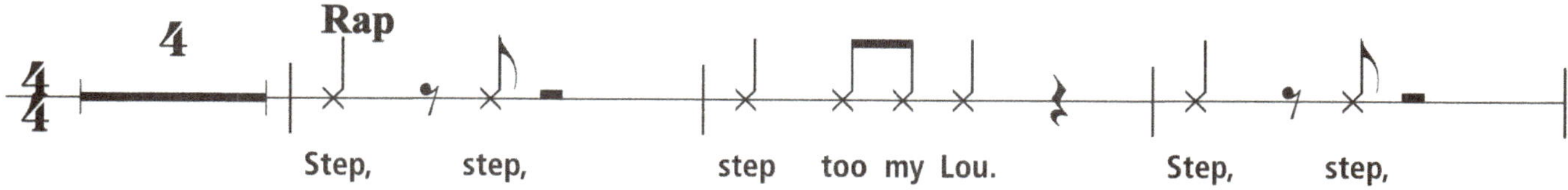

Rap
Step, step, step too my Lou. Step, step,

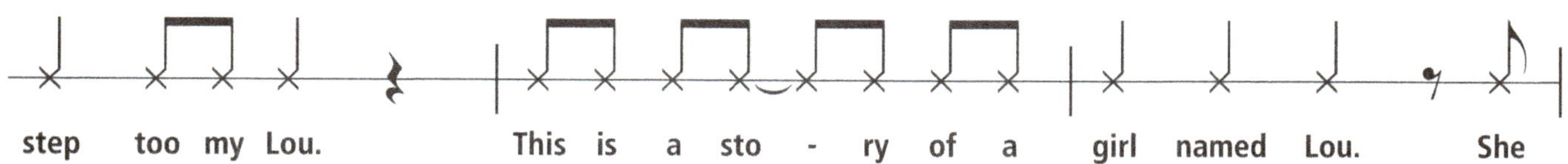

step too my Lou. This is a sto - ry of a girl named Lou. She

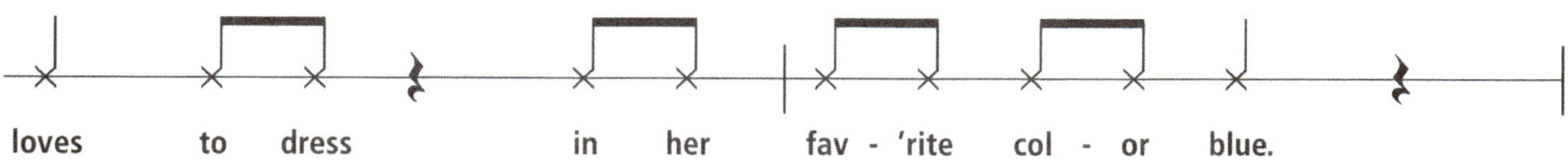

loves to dress in her fav - 'rite col - or blue.

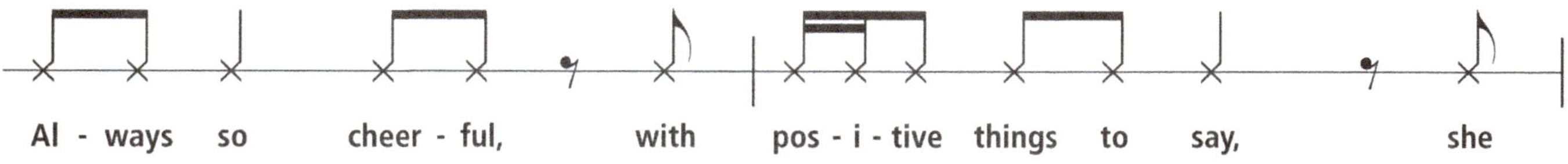

Al - ways so cheer - ful, with pos - i - tive things to say, she

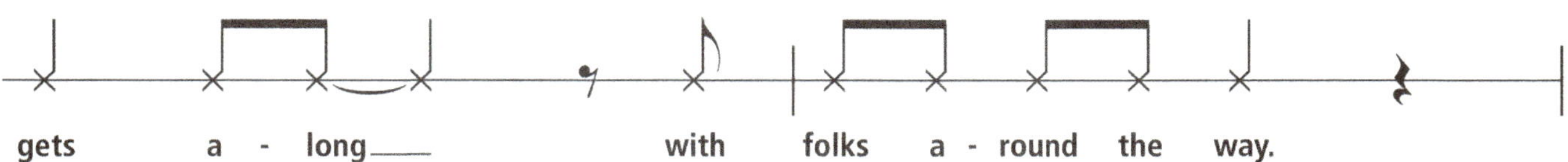

gets a - long____ with folks a - round the way.

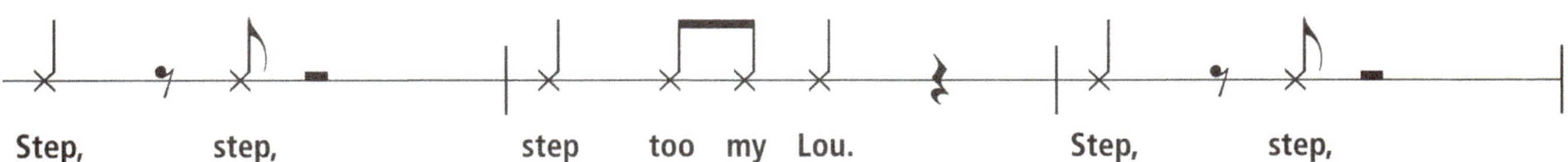

Step, step, step too my Lou. Step, step,

Step Too My Lou

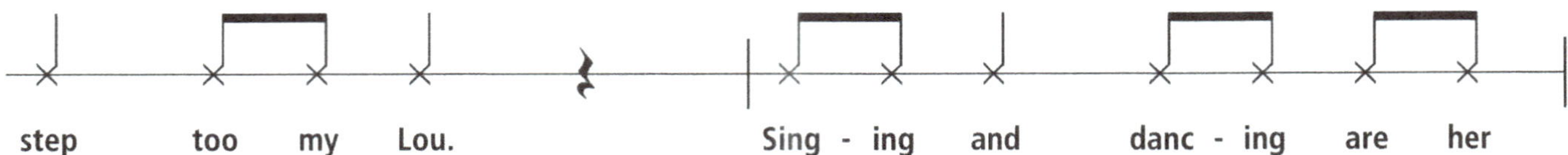

step   too   my   Lou.   Sing - ing   and   danc - ing   are   her

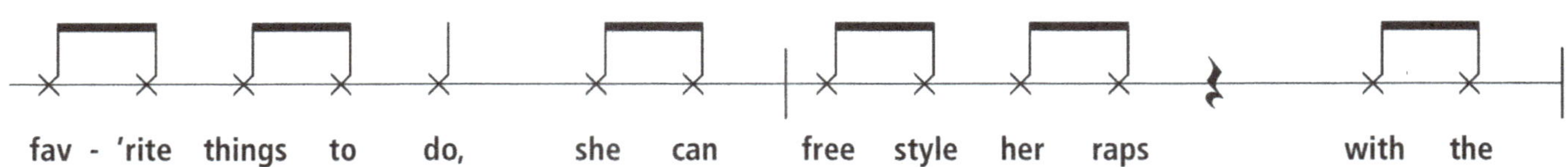

fav - 'rite   things   to   do,   she   can   free   style   her   raps   with   the

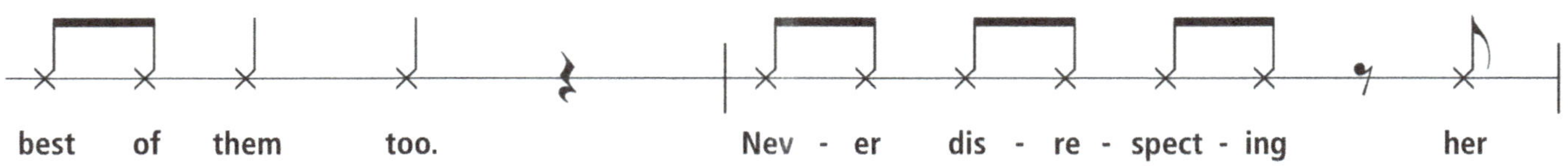

best   of   them   too.   Nev - er   dis - re - spect - ing   her

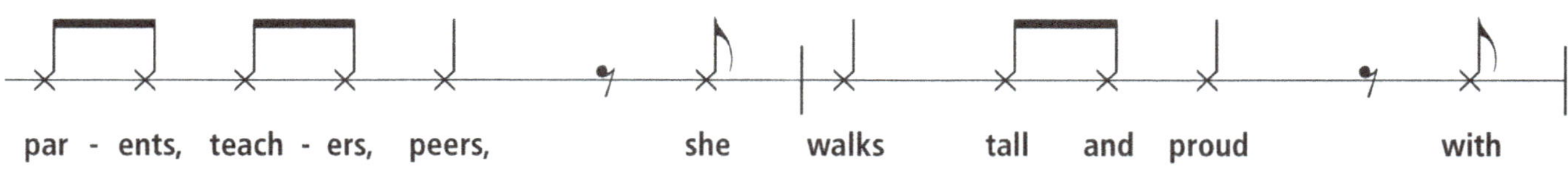

par - ents,   teach - ers,   peers,   she   walks   tall   and   proud   with

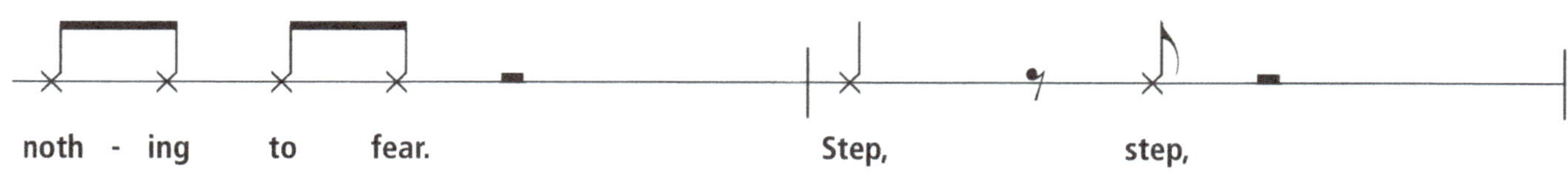

noth - ing   to   fear.   Step,   step,

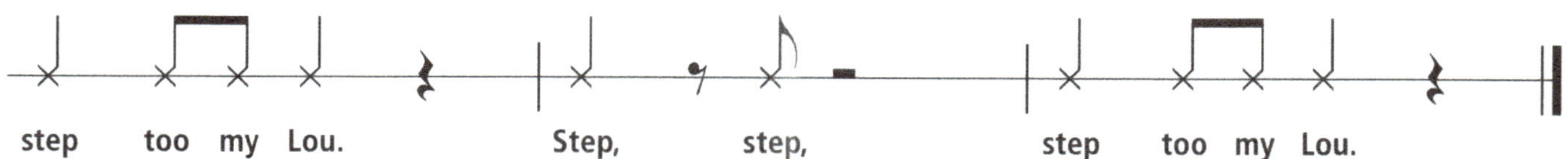

step   too   my   Lou.   Step,   step,   step   too   my   Lou.

Stille Nacht
(Silent Night)

Music by Franz Gruber
Arranged by Buryl Red
Words by Joseph Mohr

Guitar: Capo 3 G
Melody
do
Harmony
do
Stil - le Nacht, Hei - li - ge Nacht, Al - les schläft, ein - sam wacht
Si - lent night, Ho - ly night, All is calm, All is bright
Oo
Oo
Al - les schläft, ein - sam wacht
All is calm, All is bright
Nur das trau - te hoch - hei - li - ge Paar. Hol - der Kna - be im lo - cki - gen Haar,
'Round yon vir - gin moth - er and child. Ho - ly in - fant so ten - der and mild,
Oh
Oh
Schlaf in himm - lisch - er Ruh', Schlaf in himm - lisch - er Ruh'.
Sleep in heav - en - ly peace, Sleep in heav - en - ly peace.
ritard. (last time)
Schlaf, schlaf, Schlaf in himm - lisch - er Ruh'.
Sleep, sleep, Sleep in heav - en - ly peace.

St. Louis Blues

Words and Music by W.C. Handy

Swing
a
F
Bb7
F
do
1. I hate to see the ev-'nin' sun go down.
2. Feel-in' to-mor-row, like I feel to-day.
b
Bb
Bb7
F
Hate to see the ev-'nin' sun go down.
feel to-mor-row, like I feel to-day.
c
C7
Bb7
F
'Cause my ba-by, he done left this town.
I'll pack my trunk, make my get-a-way.

Swanee

Music by George Gershwin
Words by Irving Caesar

do
D   Daug   G   D
Swa - nee, How I love ya, How I love ya, My dear old Swa-nee;___
D   Daug G   A7
___ I'd give the world to be A - mong the folks in
D   A7   D   Daug
D - I - X - I - E - ven now there's some - one Wait-ing for me,
G   D
Pray-ing for me Down by the Swa - nee,_______ The folks up north
Daug G   A7   D
will see me no more___ When I get to the Swa-nee shore.___

Texas in My Soul

Words and Music by Zeb Turner and Ernest Tubb

1. A - ma - ril - lo, San An - ton', a - ny old place I call my home. I got to
2. Cor - pus Chris - ti, Del Ri - o, west of the Pe - cos or ole' Wa - co. I got to
go. I got Tex - as in my soul.
Dal - las, Fort Worth, San An - ge - lo,
Sweet - wa - ter, Beau - mont, Wi - chi - ta Falls,
Hou - ston, Aus - tin or El Pa - so. I got to go. I got Tex - as in my soul.
Port Ar - thur, Browns - ville, I hear you call.
It is there I know my pla - ces. I see on - ly smi - lin'
Where the tum - ble - weeds are grow - ing. I know that it's there I'll be
fa - ces and so. Part - ner, the rest of the world's not worth a
go - ing to stay. I've been a Tex - an since my birth,

Texas in My Soul

pound of good ole' Tex-as dirt.
no place like it on the earth.
I got to go. I got Tex-as in my soul.

I got to go. I got Tex-as in my soul.

I got to go. I got Tex-as in my soul.

There Is Love Somewhere

Traditional African American Song

do
D   A   D
1. There is love________
2. There is hope________
3. There is joy________
4. There is peace________
some - where,________ There is
G   D   A   D
love________
hope________
joy________
peace________
some - where.________ I'm gon-na
G   D   Bm   G
reach____ out________ 'til I find some.________ There is
D   A   D
love________
hope________
joy________
peace________
some - where.________

Tom Dooley

Folk Song from the United States

G
D7
do
1., 3. Hang down your head, Tom Dool - ey, Hang down your head and cry,
2. This___ time to - mor - row, Won - der___ where I'll be?
D7
G
Hang down your head, Tom Dool - ey, Poor boy, you're bound to die.
Down in some lone - some val - ley, Hang-in' from a white oak tree.

You Were on My Mind

Words and Music by Sylvia Fricker

1. When I woke up this morn - in', you were on my mind,
and you were on my mind. I got trou - bles, oh,
oh, I got wor - ries, oh, oh, I got wounds to bind.
2. So I went to the cor - ner just to ease my pain,
just to ease my pain. I got trou - bles, oh,
oh, I got wor - ries. Oh, oh, I came home a - gain.

You Were on My Mind

3. But I woke up this morn - in'__ you were on my mind__ and
you were on my mind. I got trou - bles, oh,__
oh, I got wor - ries, oh,__ oh, I got wounds to bind.__
And I got a feel - in' down_ in my shoes,__
'way down in my shoes. I got to ram - ble, oh,__
oh, I got to move on, oh,__ oh, I got to walk a - way my

You Were on My Mind

C   D7   mp   G   C
blues. _____   But I woke up this morn - in', ___   you were on my
G   C   Bm   Am7   D7sus   f
mind _____________ and you were on my mind. _____
D7   G   C   G
I got trou - bles oh, ___ oh,   I got wor - ries oh, ___
ff
C   G   Asus   F   Am7   D
oh,   I got wounds to bind. _________________

Index